Pizza & Co.

Pizza & Co.

savory tarts, focaccias and sandwiches

A Leonardo Publishing Book

pizza & Co.

Contents

Introduction	**6**
Classic Pizzas	**12**
Special Pizzas	**40**
Vegetarian Pizzas	**104**
Focaccia	**144**
Savory Tarts	**198**
Beyond Sandwiches	**284**
Cooking Techniques	**380**
Basic Tools	**388**
Index	**394**

PIZZA: A SHORT HISTORY

All around the Mediterranean basin, primitive breads have long been made from rudimentary doughs of coarsely ground wheat and water. Initially these breads were unleavened, but later they were cooked after a short rising.

Pizza's predecessors include *schiacciate* (smashed breads) and focaccias, common in Ancient Greek and Roman times, but also traced back to earlier civilizations flourishing along the Mediterranean coasts. The name pizza in fact derives from the word *pita* or *pitta*, the name for the flatbreads that were and still are made in southern Italy, Greece and the Middle East.

Modern pizza originated in Naples, and what we think of as pizza, a round crust with tomato sauce and mozzarella melting on top, originated in the city in the late 18th and early 19th centuries. In Italy, the link between pizza and the city of Naples is so strong that Italians have come to see pizza as the perfect example of how the people of Naples are masters of making do with little more than inspiration.

The recipe for pizza was successfully exported during the mass migration of Italians at the turn of the 20th century. Today in the United States, in Little Italies across the country, delicious versions of the traditional *pizza napoletana* are quite common, and some of them even surpass the Neapolitan original. From a simple, authentic expression of the popular street cuisine of Naples, pizza has become one of the world's most recognizable foods and a symbol of Italy around the globe.

Ingredients

First of all, when making pizza it is important to use the best quality all-purpose flour available. The quality of flour will determine the elasticity and softness of the dough. For best results, mix bread flour with all-

a word of advice

When using whole, canned tomatoes for pizza sauce, remember to drain them and remove the seeds, otherwise the sauce may be too liquid and make the pizza soggy. When spreading the sauce and toppings on the pizza base, leave an empty border around the edge so the characteristic crispy crust can form.

purpose flour. Bread flour is better suited for recipes with longer rising times and it has a higher protein content.

The temperature of the water used to make the dough is also of fundamental importance because it influences the fermentation and rising time. Water that is too cold will inhibit fermentation, especially in the winter. However, water that is too hot will either kill the yeast completely or speed up the fermentation too much and the dough will lose elasticity. Pizza makers and experts have determined that water should be around 72°F (22 °C) in the winter and (64°F) 18°C in the summer.

The yeast should be dissolved in water that is tepid or just warm. Using fresh cake yeast is best for pizza, however, considering its short shelf life and unpredictable outcome the recipes in this book use active dry yeast.

The tomato sauce is another important part of a delicious pizza. The traditional recipe calls for whole, canned tomatoes that are crushed or pureed and seasoned simply with salt, pepper, oregano and olive oil. Some people like to add a teaspoon of sugar to the sauce to soften the tomatoes' acidity. The sauce should be spread lightly over the pizza base before baking. In the summer months, when fresh ripe tomatoes are available, we suggest using diced fresh tomatoes instead of a cooked sauce.

FOCACCIA

While toppings and fillings may change from town to town around Italy, focaccia is a part of every region's culinary tradition. Focaccia is a simple bread dough that is seasoned with oil and salt and spread into sheets of varying thickness.

Depending on local tradition, the focaccia may be soft or crispy. Focaccia from the region of Puglia is traditionally topped with cherry tomatoes, while Ligurian focaccia is seasoned with only salt and fresh olive oil.

another idea
For a tasty variations on classic focaccia, add ½ teaspoon ground chili pepper, 1 teaspoon fennel seeds or a handful of minced sage leaves to the dough.

Regardless of its origins, focaccia makes a perfect snack any time of day and a delicious appetizer. A hearty focaccia made with olive oil and stuffed with vegetables, cheese and ham can even serve as a complete meal.

Ingredients

Focaccia may also be enriched with other ingredients. As with pizza, when making focaccia the quality and type of flour used is important, as is the correct fermentation and rising. When making focaccia, bread flour should be used at least in part so that the dough will stand up to the long rising time and puff up while baking. Once the dough has been mixed and kneaded, it must rise for at least 2 hours. To speed up the process leave the dough to rise in a warm dry place, like the oven.

For the best fermentation results, punch down the dough at least once halfway through the rising time. This will help to evenly distribute the enzymes.

SAVORY TARTS

The perfect entrée for a formal lunch or main course for a light dinner; savory tarts are convenient pot-luck or picnic dishes and can be easily transformed into appetizing finger food for brunches or cocktail parties.

This formidable dish is simple to prepare yet irresistible. The flaky crust may be topped with any number of fillings, usually with an egg or cheese base. The basic filling can be enriched with cured meats, vegetables or even smoked fish or crustaceans. There are no rules regarding the possible combinations, in fact leftovers are often used in the filling for savory tarts. Let the recipes in this book serve as guidelines to help create original meals. A savory tart, like pizza, has a correct balance of nutrients and can take the place of a sandwich or other quick meal.

a tip
When preparing pastry for savory tarts, it is important use cold butter or margarine and ice water. Remember to let the dough rest in the refrigerator; this helps the ingredients to compact and facilitates an even cooking.

Ingredients

Unsweetened puff pastry and pâté brisée are the typical doughs used for savory tart crusts. The type of pastry used depends mainly on personal taste. Puff pastry pairs well with light fillings that are not overly moist. Pâté brisée crusts should have a hearty, rich filling that will stand up to this heavier pastry. When making tarts with very light fillings, it is best to cook the crust first, lined with parchment paper and filled with dried beans or pie weights. The tart is then cooled, filled and baked a second time just long enough to cook the filling.

When short on time, it is possible to buy perfectly adequate frozen or fresh pastry bases at supermarkets or specialty stores.

BEYOND SANDWICHES

Panini, panzerotti, bruschette and piadine: simple foods that can turn a snack into an elegant feast.

A wide range of leavened and unleavened doughs are used as bases for these little snacks. The fillings and toppings can vary greatly according to taste and occasion. Choose between whole-wheat bread, flavored rolls, piadinas or focaccia for these quick and easy preparations. If the occasion calls for more elaborate or rich appetizers, experiment with delicious fried panzerotti or ravioli.

The sizes and portions of these "breads" can vary, from family-style bruschette for outdoor parties to tiny calzones and focaccias to serve as hors d'œuvres at more elegant occasions. This chapter is full of ideas that will tempt the palate.

a word of advice

If the bread becomes dry or loses flavor when making sandwiches, wrap it in a damp kitchen towel and heat it up for a few minutes in the oven.
To preserve bread, wrap it in plastic wrap and refrigerate until use.

Contents

classic pizzas 12

special pizzas 40

vegetarian pizzas 104

focaccias 144

savory tarts 198

beyond sandwiches 284

classic pizzas

Pizza

ham pizza

Ingredients for 4 servings

Dough:

1¾ tsps (12 g) active dry yeast
3/4 cup plus 1 tbsp (200 ml) warm water
salt, **1** tsp sugar
3 tbsps extra-virgin olive oil
3¼ cups (14 oz or 400 g) all-purpose flour

Topping:

6½ oz (180 g) canned whole tomatoes
salt and pepper
2 tbsps extra-virgin olive oil
8 oz (220 g) mozzarella, drained and sliced
7 oz (200 g) ham, thinly sliced

Preheat the oven to 400°F (200°C or Gas Mark 6). Prepare the pizza dough following the recipe on page 382. Puree the tomatoes with a pinch of salt and fresh ground pepper to taste.
Roll out the dough into rounds and place them on oiled baking sheets. Spread 1 tablespoon of tomato puree on each pizza, leaving a 1/2-inch (1 cm) border. Drizzle over the olive oil, making sure to coat the edge.
Cover with the mozzarella and bake for 20 minutes. Remove from the oven and top with the ham slices. Serve immediately.

For a stronger flavor, used smoked scamorza cheese in place of the mozzarella.

Preparation time **20 minutes**
Cooking time **20 minutes**
Level **easy**
Beer **Italian Lager**

four seasons pizza

Ingredients for 4 servings

Dough:

1¾ tsps (12 g) active dry yeast
3/4 cup plus 1 tbsp (200 ml) warm water
salt, **1** tsp sugar
3 tbsps extra-virgin olive oil
3¼ cups (14 oz or 400 g) all-purpose flour

Topping:

6½ oz (180 g) canned crushed tomatoes
7 oz (200 g) mozzarella, drained and sliced
10 pitted black olives, **4** slices ham, diced
2 button mushrooms, thinly sliced
6 artichokes in oil, drained and quartered
2 tbsps extra-virgin olive oil

Preheat the oven to 400°F (200°C or Gas Mark 6). Prepare the pizza dough following the recipe on page 382. Roll out the dough balls on a lightly floured work surface. Place the rounds on 4 oiled baking sheets.
Spread a spoonful of the tomatoes over the dough, leaving a 1/2-inch (1 cm) border. Cover each pizza with cheese. Cover a quarter of each pizza with olives, a quarter with mushrooms, a quarter with artichokes and a quarter with ham. Drizzle the pizzas with olive oil and bake for 25 minutes.

Add a few slices of speck, if desired, to the quarters of the pizzas topped with the mushrooms.

Preparation time **20 minutes**
Cooking time **25 minutes**
Level **easy**
Beer **Italian Lager**

prosciutto pizza

Ingredients for 4 servings

Dough:

1¾ tsps (12 g) active dry yeast

3/4 cup plus 1 tbsp (200 ml) warm water

salt, **1** tsp sugar

3 tbsps extra-virgin olive oil

3¼ cups (14 oz or 400 g) all-purpose flour

Topping:

6½ oz (180 g) canned whole tomatoes

salt

2 tbsps extra-virgin olive oil

8 oz (220 g) mozzarella, shredded

5½ oz (150 g) prosciutto, thinly sliced

Preheat the oven to 400°F (200°C or Gas Mark 6). Dissolve the yeast in the warm water. Add the salt, sugar and olive oil and mix vigorously with a spoon.
Mound the flour on a work surface and make a well in the center. Pour the yeast mixture into the well and mix to form a smooth and elastic dough. Place the dough in a large, floured mixing bowl. Cover with a clean kitchen towel and let rise about 2 hours. Punch down the dough and divide it into 4 balls. Cover and let rise for another hour. Puree the tomatoes with a little salt.
Roll out the dough into rounds and place them on oiled baking sheets. Spread a spoonful of tomato sauce on the dough, leaving a 1/2-inch (1 cm) border. Drizzle a little olive oil over the pizzas, taking care to coat the outside edge. Cover with mozzarella and bake for 20 minutes. Remove the pizzas from the oven, top with the prosciutto and serve. Alternatively, top with prosciutto and bake for 1 more minute.

▛ For a Parma-style pizza, add shaved parmesan to the pizza along with the prosciutto.

Preparation time **15 minutes**
Cooking time **20 minutes**
Level **easy**
Beer **German Pilsner**

marinara pizza

Ingredients for 4 servings

Dough:

1¾ tsps (12 g) active dry yeast

3/4 cup plus 1 tbsp (200 ml) warm water

salt, **1** tsp sugar

3 tbsps extra-virgin olive oil

3¼ cups (14 oz or 400 g) all-purpose flour

Topping:

7 oz (200 g) canned whole tomatoes

salt and pepper

3 tbsps extra-virgin olive oil

3 garlic cloves

1 bunch parsley, minced

Preheat the oven to 400°F (200°C or Gas Mark 6).
Prepare the pizza dough following the recipe on page 382.
Puree the tomatoes with a little salt and pepper.
Roll out the dough balls on a lightly floured work surface.
Place the rounds on 4 oiled baking sheets. Spread a spoonful of tomato sauce on the dough, leaving a 1/2-inch (1 cm) border. Drizzle a little olive oil over the pizzas, taking care to coat the outside edge.
Peel the garlic, remove the green shoot and thinly slice the rest of the clove. Sprinkle half the parsley and 1 sliced garlic clove over the pizza.
Bake for 15 minutes. Sprinkle over the remaining garlic and parsley and bake for another 10 minutes. Serve hot.

⌐ The parsley may be substituted with fresh basil, which will pair beautifully with the garlic.

Preparation time **15 minutes**
Cooking time **25 minutes**
Level **easy**
Beer **Czech Pilsner**

cherry tomato and mushroom pizza

Ingredients for 4 servings

Dough:

1¾ tsps (12 g) active dry yeast

3/4 cup plus 1 tbsp (200 ml) warm water

salt, **1** tsp sugar

3 tbsps extra-virgin olive oil

3¼ cups (14 oz or 400 g) all-purpose flour

Topping:

6 button mushrooms

12½ oz (350 g) buffalo mozzarella, sliced

25 cherry tomatoes, halved

2 tbsps extra-virgin olive oil

salt

oregano

Preheat the oven to 425°F (220°C or Gas Mark 7). Prepare the pizza dough following the recipe on page 382. Roll out the dough balls on a lightly floured work surface. Clean the mushrooms with a damp paper towel, peel the cap and stem and thinly slice.
Place the dough rounds on 4 lightly oiled baking sheets. Top with the mozzarella slices, and place the tomatoes and mushrooms in the empty spaces between the cheese. Drizzle with olive oil and sprinkle with salt and oregano. Bake for 15 minutes and serve hot.

Preparation time **10 minutes**
Cooking time **15 minutes**
Level **easy**
Beer **German Weizen**

Try replacing the button mushrooms with thinly sliced sautéed fresh porcini.

capricciosa pizza

Ingredients for 4 servings

Dough:

1¾ tsps (12 g) active dry yeast

3/4 cup plus 1 tbsp (200 ml) warm water

salt, **1** tsp sugar

3 tbsps extra-virgin olive oil

3¼ cups (14 oz or 400 g) all-purpose flour

Topping:

10½ oz (300 g) canned crushed tomatoes

10 artichokes in oil, drained and quartered

6 anchovy fillets in oil, drained

2½ oz (70 g) small mushrooms in oil, drained

1/3 cup (2 oz or 50 g) black olives, pitted

2 tbsps capers, salt

9 oz (250 g) mozzarella, sliced

5 tbsps extra-virgin olive oil

Preheat the oven to 425°F (220°C or Gas Mark 7). Prepare the pizza dough following the recipe on page 382. Pour the crushed tomatoes in a bowl and add 2 tablespoons of olive oil and a pinch of salt. Mix to combine. Roll out the dough balls on a lightly floured work surface. Place the rounds on 4 oiled baking sheets.
Spread a spoonful of tomato sauce on the dough, leaving a 1/2-inch (1 cm) border. Drizzle a little olive oil over the pizzas, taking care to coat the outside edge.
Top the pizza with the artichokes, anchovies, mushrooms, olives, capers, and mozzarella. Drizzle with the remaining olive oil and bake for 20 minutes. Serve immediately.

Preparation time **15 minutes**
Cooking time **20 minutes**
Level **easy**
Beer **Italian Lager**

margherita pizza

Classic Pizzas

Ingredients for 4-6 servings

Dough:

1¾ tsps (12 g) active dry yeast

3/4 cup plus 1 tbsp (200 ml) warm water

1 tsp sugar, 3 tbsps extra-virgin olive oil

3¼ cups (14 oz or 400 g) all-purpose flour, salt

Topping:

4 tomatoes, blanched, peeled and deseeded

2 tbsps extra-virgin olive oil

7 oz (200g) mozzarella, diced, salt

Garnish:

20 cherry tomatoes, quartered

fresh basil leaves

For additional flavor, add black olives, capers and a few anchovy fillets.

Preheat the oven to 400°F (200°C or Gas Mark 6). Prepare the pizza dough following the recipe on page 382. Roll out the dough balls into 1/2-inch (1/2 cm) thick rounds on a lightly floured work surface. Place the rounds on 4 oiled baking sheets.
Puree the tomatoes and dry the diced mozzarella on a paper towel. Spread a spoonful of tomato puree over the pizza rounds and top with the mozzarella.
Season with salt and bake for 20 minutes. Remove the pizzas from the oven and garnish with the cherry tomatoes and a few basil leaves. Serve immediately.

Preparation time **10 minutes**
Cooking time **20 minutes**
Level **easy**
Beer **Italian Lager**

neapolitan pizza

Ingredients for 4 servings

Dough:

1¾ tsps (12 g) active dry yeast

3/4 cup plus 1 tbsp (200 ml) warm water

salt, **1** tsp sugar

3 tbsps extra-virgin olive oil

3¼ cups (14 oz or 400 g) all-purpose flour

Topping:

7 oz (200 g) canned whole tomatoes

salt and pepper

7½ oz (220 g) mozzarella, diced

3 tbsps extra-virgin olive oil

10 anchovy fillets

Preheat the oven to 400°F (200°C or Gas Mark 6). Prepare the pizza dough following the recipe on page 382. Puree the tomatoes with a little salt and pepper. Roll out the dough balls on a lightly floured work surface. Place the rounds on 4 oiled baking sheets. Using the back of a spoon, spread a spoonful of tomato sauce over the dough, leaving a 1/2-inch (1 cm) border. Dry the mozzarella on a paper towel. Drizzle the pizzas with olive oil and then top with mozzarella and anchovy fillets. Bake for 25 minutes and serve immediately.

⌐ Try substituting cow's milk mozzarella with buffalo mozzarella. For this variation, add a few minutes onto the cooking time.

Preparation time **25 minutes**
Cooking time **25 minutes**
Level **easy**
Beer **Italian Lager**

devil's pizza

Ingredients for 4 servings

Dough:

1¾ tsps (12 g) active dry yeast

3/4 cup plus 1 tbsp (200 ml) warm water

salt, **1** tsp sugar

3 tbsps extra-virgin olive oil

3¼ cups (14 oz or 400 g) all-purpose flour

Topping:

14 oz (400 g) ready-made tomato sauce

9 oz (250) mozzarella, diced

5½ (150 g) spicy salami, peeled and sliced

extra-virgin olive oil, salt

Classic Pizzas

Preheat the oven to 425°F (220°C or Gas Mark 7). Prepare the pizza dough following the recipe on page 382. Oil 4 baking sheets and spread out a ball of dough on each baking sheet by hand. Spread the tomato sauce over the surface of the pizzas.
Bake for 10 minutes. Remove the pizzas from the oven and top with the mozzarella and salami slices. Season with salt and a pinch of oregano, if desired.
Drizzle with olive oil and bake for another 10-15 minutes.

For an even spicier pizza, substitute the hot salami with 3½ oz (100 g) of Calabrian 'nduja salami.

Preparation time **15 minutes**
Cooking time **25 minutes**
Level **easy**
Beer **Italian Lager**

sausage and mushroom pizza

Ingredients for 4 servings

Dough:

1¾ tsps (12 g) active dry yeast
3/4 cup plus 1 tbsp (200 ml) warm water
salt, **1** tsp sugar
3 tbsps extra-virgin olive oil
3¼ cups (14 oz or 400 g) all-purpose flour

Topping:

6½ oz (180 g) canned whole tomatoes
salt and pepper
8 oz (220 g) mozzarella, shredded
2 sausages, casings removed
6 button mushrooms, cleaned and sliced
3 tbsps extra-virgin olive oil

Preheat the oven to 425°F (220°C or Gas Mark 7). Prepare the pizza dough following the recipe on page 382. Puree the tomatoes with a little salt and pepper. Roll out the dough balls on a lightly floured work surface. Place the rounds on 4 oiled baking sheets. Using the back of a spoon, spread a spoonful of tomato sauce over the dough, leaving a 1/2-inch (1 cm) border. Break up the sausages into small pieces.
Top the pizza with mozzarella and sausage pieces. Add the mushrooms and season with pinches of salt and pepper. Drizzle with olive oil and bake for 25 minutes. Serve immediately.

For an elegant touch, drizzle this pizza with a little truffle oil before serving.

Preparation time **20 minutes**
Cooking time **25 minutes**
Level **easy**
Beer **English Ale**

mixed seafood pizza

Ingredients for 4 servings

Dough:

4 tsps (25 g) active dry yeast

ground saffron, salt

1 cup (250 ml) warm water

4 cups (1 lb plus 1½ oz or 500 g) all-purpose flour

Topping:

1 lb 1½ oz (500 g) clams

1 lb (450 g) mussels, **1** garlic clove

1/2 cup (120 ml) white wine

1 tbsp minced parsley, salt and pepper

10½ oz (300 g) shrimp, shelled and deveined

2 bay leaves, **2** squid, cleaned

4 baby octopus, cleaned

5 tbsps extra-virgin olive oil

10½ oz (300 g) tomato sauce

6 zucchini flowers, sliced

Dissolve the yeast, saffron and a pinch of salt in the warm water. Sift the flour onto a work surface, make a well in the center and add the yeast mixture. Mix to obtain a rough dough, and then knead with the hands until smooth. Cover and let rest in a warm place for 1 hour. Wash the clams under cold running water and then soak for at least 20 minutes. Wash and de-beard the mussels. Cook the clams and the mussels in a frying pan with the garlic clove, half of the wine and the parsley and season with salt and pepper. Remove the shells from most of the clams and mussels. Preheat the oven to 425°F (220°C or Gas Mark 7). Blanch the shrimp for 1 minute in 2 cups (500 ml) of water, the remaining wine and 1 bay leaf. In a saucepan, boil the baby octopus and the squid with the remaining bay leaf for 20 minutes. Drain and cut into small pieces. Add to the shrimp, season with a pinch of salt and drizzle with olive oil. Toss to coat. Divide the pizza dough into 4 balls. Roll out each ball of dough and place on an oiled baking sheet. Spread the pizzas with a spoonful of tomato sauce, season with salt and drizzle with olive oil. Top with the seafood and bake for 20 minutes. Remove from the oven, sprinkle over the zucchini flowers and cook for another 5 minutes.

Preparation time **35 minutes**
Cooking time **35 minutes**
Level **medium**
Wine **Bianco d'Alcamo**

white pizza with anchovies and capers

Ingredients for 4 servings

Dough:

1 ¾ tsps (12 g) active dry yeast

3/4 cup plus 1 tbsp (200 ml) warm water

salt, **1** tsp sugar

3 tbsps extra-virgin olive oil

3 ¼ cups (14 oz or 400 g) all-purpose flour

Topping:

10-12 anchovies packed in salt

2 tbsps capers in vinegar

extra-virgin olive oil

pepper

Preheat the oven to 425°F (220°C or Gas Mark 7). Prepare the pizza dough following the recipe on page 382. Wash the anchovies, remove any bones and break them up into small pieces.
Roll out the dough balls on a lightly floured work surface. Place the rounds on 4 oiled baking sheets.
Drain the capers, rinse them under running water and sprinkle over the pizzas. Top with the anchovies, season with salt and drizzle with olive oil if desired.
Bake for 20-25 minutes and season with freshly ground pepper before serving.

This pizza can be enriched by the addition of quartered cherry tomatoes, oregano and fresh parsley.

Preparation time **15 minutes**
Cooking time **25 minutes**
Level **easy**
Wine **Cirò Rosato**

four cheese pizza

Ingredients for 4 servings

Dough:

1¾ tsps (12 g) active dry yeast

3/4 cup plus 1 tbsp (200 ml) warm water

salt, **1** tsp sugar

3 tbsps extra-virgin olive oil

3¼ cups (14 oz or 400 g) all-purpose flour

Topping:

3½ oz (100 g) mozzarella, diced

3½ oz (100 g) fontina cheese, diced

3 oz (80 g) Gorgonzola cheese, diced

1/2 cup (2 oz or 50 g) grated Parmesan cheese

extra-virgin olive oil

salt and pepper

Preheat the oven to 400°F (200°C or Gas Mark 6). Prepare the pizza dough following the recipe on page 382. Lightly flour a large work surface and roll the balls of dough into rounds using a rolling pin. Place the pizzas on an oiled baking sheet. Top them with the mozzarella, fontina and Gorgonzola and sprinkle with Parmesan. Season with salt and pepper. Bake the pizzas for 20-25 minutes and serve hot.

Preparation time **15 minutes**
Cooking time **25 minutes**
Level **easy**
Beer **Irish Stout**

special pizzas

Pizza

pizza bianca

Ingredients for 4 servings

Dough:

1¾ tsps (12 g) active dry yeast
3/4 cup plus 1 tbsp (200 ml) warm water
salt, **1** tsp sugar
3 tbsps extra-virgin olive oil
3¼ cups (14 oz or 400 g) all-purpose flour

Pesto:

1 tbsp toasted pine nuts, ½ garlic clove
6 cups (5½ oz or 150 g) basil leaves
7 tbsps extra-virgin olive oil
2 tbsps grated Parmesan, salt

Topping:

2 cups (7 oz or 200 g) green beans, trimmed
9 oz (250 g) crescenza or other creamy, melting cheese, diced
7 oz (200 g) mozzarella, diced
2 tbsps extra-virgin olive oil, salt

Preheat the oven to 400°F (200°C or Gas Mark 6).
Prepare the pizza dough following the recipe on page 382.
Roll out the dough balls on a lightly floured work surface.
Place the rounds on 4 oiled baking sheets. Cover and let rise for 20-25 minutes.
Meanwhile, make the pesto: Blend the pine nuts, garlic, and salt in a food processor or a mortar and pestle.
Add the basil and drizzle over the olive oil and Parmesan.
Blend to form a smooth sauce.
Boil the green beans in salted water for 15 minutes.
Drain and cut into 1-inch (2½ cm) lengths.
Top the pizza with the crescenza and mozzarella.
Bake for 25 minutes. Remove from the oven, sprinkle over the green beans and top with the pesto.
Serve immediately.

Preparation time **15 minutes**
Cooking time **40 minutes**
Level **easy**
Wine **Riviera Ligure di Ponente Pigato**

bologna-style calzone

Ingredients for 4 servings

Dough:

1¾ tsps (12 g) active dry yeast
3/4 cup plus 1 tbsp (200 ml) warm water
salt, **1** tsp sugar
3 tbsps extra-virgin olive oil
3¼ cups (14 oz or 400 g) all-purpose flour

Filling:

1 cup (250 ml) tomato sauce
14 oz (400 g) mozzarella
7 oz (200 g) mortadella, thinly sliced
salt
3 tbsps extra-virgin olive oil

Preheat the oven to 400°F (200°C or Gas Mark 6).
Prepare the pizza dough following the recipe on page 382. Roll out the dough on a lightly floured surface into 4 thin discs, about 10 inches (24 cm) in diameter.
Place the rounds on lightly oiled baking sheets.
Spread half of each dough round with tomato sauce, top with the mozzarella and mortadella and season with salt. Fold the dough in half to form a half-moon shape and pinch around the edge to close. Brush the top of each calzone with olive oil and bake for 25 minutes.
Serve very hot.

Make smaller calzone and fry them to serve as an appetizer. The filling may be changed as desired for a wider variety of flavors.

Preparation time **15 minutes**
Cooking time **25 minutes**
Level **easy**
Beer **Italian Lager**

carpaccio pizza with bresaola and salad

Ingredients for 4 servings

Dough:

1¾ tsps (12 g) active dry yeast

3/4 cup plus 1 tbsp (200 ml) warm water

salt, **1** tsp sugar

3 tbsps extra-virgin olive oil

3¼ cups (14 oz or 400 g) all-purpose flour

Topping:

1 head of butter lettuce, shredded

salt and pepper

3 tbsps extra-virgin olive oil

7 oz (200 g) bresaola, thinly sliced

9 oz (250 g) Parmesan cheese, shaved

Preheat the oven to 400°F (200°C or Gas Mark 6). Prepare the pizza dough following the recipe on page 382. Roll out the dough on a lightly floured surface into 4 thin discs, about 10 inches (24 cm) in diameter and about 3 mm thick. Place the rounds on lightly oiled baking sheets and bake for 10 minutes.
Season the lettuce with pinches of salt and pepper and drizzle with 2 tablespoons olive oil.
Remember to dress the salad just before use so it doesn't lose flavor or its crunchy texture.
Remove the pizzas from the oven. Top with the dressed lettuce, the bresaola and Parmesan cheese shavings.

For a variation, use prosciutto instead of bresaola and arugula or radicchio in place of the lettuce. Or try replacing the bresaola with smoked swordfish.

Preparation time **15 minutes**
Cooking time **10 minutes**
Level **easy**
Beer **German Weizen**

pear and gorgonzola pizza

Ingredients for 4 servings

Dough:

1¾ tsps (12 g) active dry yeast
3/4 cup plus 1 tbsp (200 ml) warm water
salt, **1** tsp sugar
3 tbsps extra-virgin olive oil
3¼ cups (14 oz or 400 g) all-purpose flour

Topping:

9 oz (250 g) Gorgonzola cheese, diced
7 oz (200 g) mozzarella, thinly sliced
2 pears, peeled, cored and thinly sliced
salt and pepper
2 tbsps extra-virgin olive oil

Preheat the oven to 400°F (200°C or Gas Mark 6). Prepare the pizza dough following the recipe on page 382. Roll out the dough on a lightly floured surface into 4 thin discs, about 9 inches (22 cm) in diameter and about 1/5-inch (3 mm) thick. Place the rounds on lightly oiled baking sheets and bake for 10 minutes.
Top the pizzas with the two kinds of cheese and the pear slices. Season with freshly ground pepper and a pinch of salt and drizzle with olive oil. Bake for 20-25 minutes. Serve immediately.

Special Pizzas

For additional flavor, add chopped walnuts to this pizza or substitute the pears with sautéed spinach, zucchini or artichokes.

Preparation time **15 minutes**
Cooking time **25 minutes**
Level **easy**
Beer **German Weizen**

white pizza with asparagus and bottarga

Ingredients for 4 servings

Dough:

1¾ tsps (12 g) active dry yeast

3/4 cup plus 1 tbsp (200 ml) warm water

salt, **1** tsp sugar

3 tbsps extra-virgin olive oil

3¼ cups (14 oz or 400 g) all-purpose flour

Topping:

1 lb (450 g) asparagus

1 shallot, minced

5 tbsps extra-virgin olive oil, salt

1/2 cup (120 ml) heavy cream

2 oz (60 g) tuna bottarga (see note)

12½ oz (350 g) mozzarella, diced

Prepare the pizza dough following the recipe on page 382. Preheat the oven to 400°F (200°C or Gas Mark 6). Trim the asparagus and cut the tips from the stalks, and slice the stalks into rounds. Blanch the tips in boiling salted water until tender. Drain and set aside. Sauté the shallot in 1 tablespoon of olive oil, add the asparagus rounds and a little water.
Cook, covered, for 10-15 minutes. Puree the asparagus rounds with the cream in a blender or food processor and season to taste with salt. Grate the tuna bottarga into a bowl and drizzle over 2 tablespoons olive oil.
Place the diced mozzarella on a paper towel to absorb any excess liquid. Roll out the dough on a lightly floured surface into 4 thin discs, about 1/5-inch (3 mm) thick.
Place the rounds on lightly oiled baking sheets.
Spread the asparagus cream over the pizzas and top with the mozzarella. Drizzle over the bottarga and olive oil mixture. Place the asparagus tips over the pizzas and bake for 25 minutes. Serve very hot.

Bottarga is cured fish roe with a strong, salty flavor. It could be replaced here with anchovies.

Preparation time **20 minutes**
Cooking time **40 minutes**
Level **easy**
Wine **Torbato di Alghero**

summer kamut pizza

Ingredients for 4 servings

Dough:

1 tsp (8 g) active dry yeast
1/2 cup (125 ml) warm water
1¼ cups (5½ oz or 150 g) all-purpose flour
3/4 cup plus 1 tbsp (3½ oz or 100 g) kamut flour
2 tbsps extra-virgin olive oil, salt

Topping:

4 tomatoes, sliced
9 oz (250 g) crescenza or other creamy, melting cheese
3 (10 ½ oz or 300 g) baby zucchini with flowers attached
fresh basil leaves, salt and pepper
4 tbsps extra-virgin olive oil

Kamut is an ancient grain, a predecessor to modern durum wheat. It was discovered thousands of years ago in the Middle East, and is currently enjoying a newfound popularity.

Dissolve the yeast in the water. Mix together the two kinds of flour and mound them on a work surface, making a well at the center. Add the olive oil, a pinch of salt and the yeast mixture to the well.
Mix to form a rough dough and then knead until smooth. Let rise in a warm place for 1 hour.
Preheat the oven to 400°F (200°C or Gas Mark 6).
Roll out the dough into 4 rounds and place them on 4 oiled baking sheets. Top the pizzas with the tomato slices.
Drop spoonfuls of crescenza onto the pizzas.
Slice the zucchini very thinly or with a mandolin and julienne the zucchini flowers.
Place in a bowl and season with 2 tablespoons olive oil, salt and pepper. iSpoon the zucchini mixture over the pizzas and spread into even layers. Tear the basil leaves into small pieces and sprinkle them over the pizzas.
Drizzle with olive oil and bake for 25 minutes.

Preparation time **20 minutes**
Cooking time **25 minutes**
Level **easy**
Beer **English Lager**

pizza with pecorino, fresh porcini and ham

Ingredients for 4 servings

Dough:

1½ tsps active dry yeast

1 cup minus 1 tbsp (220 ml) water

3⅔ cups (1 lb or 450 g) all-purpose flour

4 tbsps extra-virgin olive oil

3 tsps salt

Topping:

9 oz (250 g) cow's milk mozzarella, diced

10½ oz (300 g) fresh porcini mushrooms, thinly sliced

extra-virgin olive oil, salt and pepper

3/4 cup (7 oz or 200 g) ready-made tomato sauce

1 cup (3½ oz or 100 g) grated aged pecorino cheese

7 oz (200 g) smoked ham, thinly sliced

For a tasty alternative, try replacing the tomato sauce with sliced fresh tomatoes

Dissolve the yeast in half of the water. Mound the flour on a work surface and make a well in the center. Pour the yeast mixture into the well and add the remaining water, olive oil and salt. Mix to form a dough and knead until smooth and elastic. Roll the dough into a ball and place in a floured bowl. Cover and let rise at room temperature for 1 hour 30 minutes.
Preheat the oven to 400°F (200°C or Gas Mark 6). Divide the dough into quarters and roll out each quarter into a thin round.
Place the pizza rounds on an oiled baking sheet. Lay the mozzarella on a paper towel to absorb any excess moisture. Mix together the mushrooms with pinches of salt and pepper and a drizzle of olive oil.
Top the pizzas with the tomato sauce, mozzarella, pecorino and finally the mushroom mixture.
Bake for about 20 minutes and remove from the oven. Top each pizza with a slice of smoked ham and serve.

Preparation time **25 minutes**
Cooking time **20 minutes**
Level **easy**
Beer **Italian Lager**

calabrian-style pizza with 'ndjua

Ingredients for 4 servings

Dough:

1¾ tsps (12 g) active dry yeast

3/4 cup plus 1 tbsp (200 ml) warm water

salt, **1** tsp sugar

3 tbsps extra-virgin olive oil

3¼ cups (14 oz or 400 g) all-purpose flour

Topping:

2 sweet red onions, very thinly sliced

2 tbsps extra-virgin olive oil, salt

7 oz (200 g) buffalo mozzarella, diced

1 cup (7 oz or 200 g) crushed tomatoes

5½ oz (150 g) 'nduja salami (see note)

Preheat oven to 400°F (200°C or Gas Mark 6).
Prepare the pizza dough following the recipe on page 382.
Roll out the dough and then place it in a well-oiled round baking pan. Cover and let rise for 25 minutes.
Mix the onions with salt and the olive oil.
Dry the mozzarella with paper towels.
Top the pizza with crushed tomatoes, the onions, the mozzarella and the 'nduja, broken into pieces.
Bake for around 20 minutes. Serve hot.

⌐ 'Nduja is a very spicy, soft, spreadable cured pork from Calabria. It could be replaced here with another spicy salami or sausage.

Preparation time **10 minutes**
Cooking time **20 minutes**
Level **easy**
Beer **Belgian Trappist**

smoked salmon pizza

Ingredients for 4 servings

Dough:

1¾ tsps (12 g) active dry yeast
3/4 cup plus 1 tbsp (200 ml) warm water
salt, **1** tsp sugar
3 tbsps extra-virgin olive oil
3¼ cups (14 oz or 400 g) all-purpose flour

Topping:

5 cups (5½ oz or 150 g) fresh spinach
10½ oz (300 g) crescenza or other creamy, melting cheese
7 tbsps heavy cream, salt and pepper
6 oz (160 g) smoked salmon, thinly sliced

Prepare the pizza dough following the recipe on page 382. Preheat oven to 400°F (200°C or Gas Mark 6). Blanch the spinach leaves in boiling salted water for 1 minute. Drain and squeeze out the excess water. Set aside. Roll out the dough on a lightly floured surface into 4 thin discs, about 9 inches (22 cm) in diameter and 3 mm thick. Place the rounds on lightly oiled baking sheets. Beat the crescenza cheese with 5 tablespoons of cream and season to taste with salt and pepper. Spread the cheese mixture on the pizzas.
Top with the smoked salmon slices and the blanched spinach. Drizzle over the remaining cream and season with freshly ground pepper if desired.
Bake for 25 minutes.

Smoking is one of the classic methods for preserving salmon. It is usually cold smoked over different types of wood such as oak and elm, with mixed herbs added for extra flavor.

Preparation time **20 minutes**
Cooking time **25 minutes**
Level **easy**
Beer **Irish Stout**

marinated octopus pizza

Ingredients for 4 servings

Dough:

1¾ tsps (12 g) active dry yeast
3/4 cup plus 1 tbsp (200 ml) warm water
salt, **1** tsp sugar
3 tbsps extra-virgin olive oil
3¼ cups (14 oz or 400 g) all-purpose flour

Topping:

2½ lb (1¼ kg) octopus
1/2 celery stick, coarsely chopped
1/2 onion, coarsely chopped
5 tbsps extra-virgin olive oil
salt and pepper
14 oz (400 g) tomatoes, thinly sliced
fresh basil leaves

Prepare the pizza dough following the recipe on page 382. Preheat oven to 400°F (200°C or Gas Mark 6).
Boil the octopus with the celery and onion in salted water until tender. Let the octopus cool in the cooking water and drain. Thinly slice the octopus and place in a bowl. Season with a pinch of salt and freshly ground pepper and drizzle with olive oil.
Spread the sliced tomatoes onto a large plate and season with a generous pinch of salt and drizzle with olive oil.
Roll out the dough on a lightly floured surface into 4 thin discs, about 1/5-inch (3 mm) thick. Place the rounds on lightly oiled baking sheets and bake for 10 minutes. Remove from heat, place the pizzas on plates and top with the tomato slices and the octopus. Sprinkle over the basil leaves and drizzle with olive oil.
Serve immediately.

Preparation time **15 minutes**
Cooking time **25 minutes**
Level **easy**
Wine **Fiano di Avellino**

pizza marinara with mussels

Ingredients for 4 servings

Dough:

1¾ tsps (12 g) active dry yeast

3/4 cup plus 1 tbsp (200 ml) warm water

salt, **1** tsp sugar

3 tbsps extra-virgin olive oil

3¼ cups (14 oz or 400 g) all-purpose flour

Topping:

4 tbsps extra-virgin olive oil

1½ lb (700 g) mussels, debearded and scrubbed

1/2 cup (120 ml) white wine

10½ oz (300 g) canned peeled whole tomatoes

2 tbsps chopped parsley

salt and pepper

2 garlic cloves, thinly sliced

For a heartier version, boil 2 small potatoes for 10 minutes, peel and thinly slice and lay over the pizza before baking.

Dissolve the yeast in half of the water. Mound the flour on a work surface and make a well in the center. Add the yeast mixture to the well along with the remaining water, oil and salt. Mix to form a smooth dough. Transfer the dough to a floured mixing bowl, cover and let rise for 1 hour 30 minutes. Preheat the oven to 400°F (200°C or Gas Mark 6). Meanwhile, place the mussels in a large frying pan with 1 tablespoon of oil. Pour over the white wine, cover and cook over medium heat until all of the mussels have opened. Remove nearly all of the mussels from the shells and return them to the cooking liquid. Blend the tomatoes with 1½ tablespoons of olive oil, the parsley and pinches of salt and pepper. Divide the dough in half and roll out each half into a thin round. Place the rounds on oiled baking sheets and top with the tomato sauce. Sprinkle over the garlic slices and the drained mussels. Drizzle with olive oil and bake for 15-20 minutes. Serve immediately.

Preparation time **30 minutes**
Cooking time **30 minutes**
Level **easy**
Beer **Italian Lager**

olive and onion pizza

Ingredients for 4 servings

Dough:

1 tsp (8 g) active dry yeast

1/2 cup (120 ml) warm water, salt

1/2 tsp sugar

4 tbsps extra-virgin olive oil

1¾ cups plus 2 tbsps (8½ oz or 240 g) all-purpose flour

1/2 cup (3½ oz or 100 g) semolina

Topping:

8 salted anchovies

1 lb (500 g) canned whole tomatoes

6 tbsps extra-virgin olive oil

2 onions, thinly sliced

salt and pepper

4 basil leaves, chopped

2 tbsps black olives in brine

Prepare the pizza dough following the recipe on page 382. Add the semolina and 2 tablespoons olive oil to the dough and mix well. Cover and let rest for 30 minutes. Preheat oven to 425°F (220°C or Gas Mark 7). Meanwhile, rinse the anchovies, remove any scales and break into small pieces. Drain the tomatoes and break them into pieces.
Heat 2 tablespoons of olive oil in a medium-sized saucepan and add the 1 onion. Brown briefly and add the tomatoes, pinches of salt and pepper and the chopped basil. Continue cooking over low heat until the sauce thickens slightly. Add the anchovies and remove from heat, continuing to stir for another 5 minutes.
Oil a large round baking sheet and place the dough in the center. Spread the dough into the pan, pushing with fingertips, until the dough covers the entire pan and edges. Fold in the extra dough to form a thicker border around the pizza's edge. Pour the tomato sauce over the pizza and top with the olives and remaining sliced onion. Bake for 30 minutes, until the crust is golden brown.

Preparation time **30 minutes**
Cooking time **45 minutes**
Level **easy**
Beer **Italian Lager**

radicchio and scamorza calzone

Ingredients for 4 servings

Dough:

1¾ tsps (12 g) active dry yeast

3/4 cup plus 1 tbsp (200 ml) warm water

salt, **1** tsp sugar

3 tbsps extra-virgin olive oil

3¼ cups (14 oz or 400 g) all-purpose flour

Topping:

3 tbsps extra-virgin olive oil

2 heads radicchio, thinly sliced

7 oz (200 g) ricotta, salt

9 oz (250 g) smoked scamorza or other mild, smoked cheese, chopped

Calzones may be made with a wide variety of fillings. We suggest a mix of bell peppers and porcini mushrooms or leeks and spinach. The dough may also be made replacing some of the all-purpose flour with whole-wheat flour for a more nutritious meal.

Prepare the pizza dough following the recipe on page 382. Preheat the oven to 400°F (200°C or Gas Mark 6). Heat 2 tablespoons of olive oil in a non-stick frying pan and add the radicchio. Season to taste with salt and sauté until tender. Mix the ricotta with a pinch of salt. Roll out the dough on a lightly floured surface into 4 thin discs, about 9 inches (22 cm) in diameter and ⅛-inch (3 mm) thick. Place the rounds on lightly oiled baking sheets. Spread a spoonful of the ricotta filling over half of the dough and top with the radicchio, then sprinkle over the scamorza. Fold the dough over the filling to make a half-moon shape. Pinch the edges of the calzones to seal. Brush with olive oil and bake for 25 minutes. Remove from the oven and serve immediately.

Preparation time **15 minutes**
Cooking time **25 minutes**
Level **easy**
Wine **Cirò Rosato**

tyrolean pizza

Ingredients for 4 servings

Dough:

3¼ tsp (25 g) active dry yeast

warm water

4 cups plus 1 tbsp (1 lb 1½ oz or 500 g) organic whole-wheat flour

2 tbsps extra-virgin olive oil, salt

Topping:

3 tbsps extra-virgin olive oil

2¼ cups (7 oz or 200 g) thinly sliced leeks

10½ oz (300 g) mascarpone

salt and pepper

9 oz (250 g) speck, thinly sliced

Dissolve the yeast in a little warm water.
Pour the flour onto a work surface and make a well at the center. Pour the yeast mixture into the well and add the olive oil and salt. Mix together with hands, adding enough water to make a smooth and pliable dough.
Form the dough into a ball, cover and let rise for 1 hour 30 minutes.
Preheat the oven to 400°F (200°C or Gas Mark 6).
Heat the olive oil in a frying pan and add the leeks. Season with a pinch of salt and cook over low heat until softened.
Roll out the dough into 4 rounds, ⅛-inch (3 mm) thick, leaving a thick edge.
Place the rounds on 4 oiled baking sheets. Beat the mascarpone with a spoon, season with salt and pepper and spread it over of the pizzas. Top with the leeks and drizzle with olive oil.
Bake the pizzas for 20 minutes. Remove from the oven, top with the speck and serve.

Preparation time **20 minutes**
Cooking time **25 minutes**
Level **easy**
Beer **German Weizen**

For a lighter version of this pizza, use ricotta in place of the mascarpone.

prosciutto and artichoke pizza

Ingredients for 4 servings

Dough:

1¾ tsps (12 g) active dry yeast

3/4 cup plus 1 tbsp (200 ml) warm water

salt, **1** tsp sugar

3 tbsps extra-virgin olive oil

3¼ cups (14 oz or 400 g) all-purpose flour

Topping:

10½ oz (300 g) canned whole tomatoes, deseeded and chopped

3½ oz (100 g) mozzarella, diced

2 oz (60 g) prosciutto, thinly sliced

3½ oz (100 g) artichokes in oil, drained and quartered

oregano, salt and pepper

6 tbsps extra-virgin olive oil

Prepare the pizza dough following the recipe on page 382. Oil the dough with 2 tablespoons of olive oil and knead for 1 minute. Let rest for 1 hour in a cool place.
Puree the tomatoes.
Preheat the oven to 425°F (220°C or Gas Mark 7).
Roll out the dough into a ¼-inch (½ cm) thick round. Place it on an oiled baking sheet and spread over the tomato puree.
Top with mozzarella, the prosciutto slices and the artichokes. Season with pinches of oregano, salt and pepper. Drizzle over the olive oil and bake for 30 minutes. Serve immediately.

Preparation time **20 minutes**
Cooking time **30 minutes**
Level **easy**
Beer **Czech Pilsner**

russian pizza

Ingredients for 4 servings

Dough:

1 tsp (8 g) active dry yeast

1/2 cup (120 ml) warm water

1 cup plus 3 tbsps (5½ oz or 150 g) all-purpose flour

3/4 cup plus 1 tbsp (3½ oz or 100 g) buckwheat flour

2 tbsps extra-virgin olive oil, salt

Topping:

9 oz (250 g) mascarpone, salt

6½ oz (180 g) smoked salmon, thinly sliced and julienned

2 tbsps extra-virgin olive oil

2 bunches arugula, coarsely chopped

fresh dill, minced

1 oz (30 g) red lumpfish roe

Dissolve the yeast in a little warm water.
Mix together the different flours and pour them onto a work surface, making a well in the center. Add the yeast mixture, olive oil, remaining water and a pinch of salt. Mix together to form a smooth dough. Let rise for at least 1 hour.
Preheat the oven to 400°F (200°C or Gas Mark 6).
Roll out the dough into 4 rounds, about 9 inches (22 cm) in diameter. Place the rounds on lightly oiled baking sheets and spread a thin layer of mascarpone over each one. Season with salt and top with the smoked salmon. Drizzle with olive oil and bake for 25 minutes.
Remove the pizzas from the oven and top with the arugula, dill and roe.

Preparation time **15 minutes**
Cooking time **25 minutes**
Level **easy**
Wine **Prosecco di Conegliano e Valdobbiadene Brut**

genoa-style calzone

Ingredients for 4 servings

Dough:

1¾ tsps (12 g) active dry yeast

3/4 cup plus 1 tbsp (200 ml) warm water

salt, **1** tsp sugar

3 tbsps extra-virgin olive oil

3¼ cups (14 oz or 400 g) all-purpose flour

Topping:

10½ oz (300 g) ricotta, salt

10½ oz (300 g) artichokes in oil, drained and sliced

2 tbsps pesto

2 tbsps extra-virgin olive oil

Prepare the pizza dough following the recipe on page 382.
Roll the dough into a ball and let rise for 1 hour 30 minutes.
Preheat the oven to 400°F (200°C or Gas Mark 6).
Sieve the ricotta and mix in the artichokes and pesto.
Season to taste with salt.
Roll out the dough into 4 thin rounds, about 10 inches (24 cm) in diameter. Spread the ricotta mixture over half of each round and fold over to form a half-moon shape. Pinch the edges of the calzones to close and brush with olive oil. Bake for 20-25 minutes.
Remove from the oven and serve immediately.

⌐ To make the pesto at home blend 1 tablespoon of pine nuts with a pinch of salt and ½ garlic clove. Add 2 handfuls of basil leaves, 2 tablespoons of grated Parmesan and drizzle in 7 tablespoons extra-virgin olive oil. Blend to combine.

Preparation time **15 minutes**
Cooking time **25 minutes**
Level **easy**
Wine **Riviera Ligure di Ponente Pigato**

potato and pancetta pizza

Ingredients for 4 servings

Dough:
1¾ tsps (12 g) active dry yeast
3/4 cup plus 1 tbsp (200 ml) warm water
salt, **1** tsp sugar
3 tbsps extra-virgin olive oil
3¼ cups (14 oz or 400 g) all-purpose flour

Topping:
1 lb (500 g) potatoes
salt and pepper
10½ oz (300 g) mild pancetta, thinly sliced
sage

Preheat the oven to 400°F (200°C or Gas Mark 6). Prepare the pizza dough following the recipe on page 382. Roll out the dough on a lightly floured surface into 4 thin rounds. Place the rounds on lightly oiled baking sheets, season with pinches of salt and drizzle with olive oil. Bake for 10 minutes. Boil the potatoes in lightly salted water until tender. Drain and let cool.
Peel the potatoes and mash them with a potato ricer directly onto the cooked pizza crusts. Season with salt and freshly ground pepper and drizzle with olive oil. Top with the pancetta slices and a few sage leaves and serve.

Special Pizzas

Adding potato and pancetta to the already cooked pizza crust gives a crunchy base and soft toppings.

Preparation time **15 minutes**
Cooking time **10 minutes**
Level **easy**
Beer **English Pale Ale**

tuna and potato pizza

Ingredients for 4 servings

Dough:

1¾ tsps (12 g) active dry yeast

3/4 cup plus 1 tbsp (200 ml) warm water

salt, **1** tsp sugar

3 tbsps extra-virgin olive oil

3¼ cups (14 oz or 400 g) all-purpose flour

Topping:

4 medium potatoes, salt

8 oz (220 g) tuna in oil, drained and crumbled

1 tbsp capers packed in salt, rinsed

2 tbsps extra-virgin olive oil

Prepare the pizza dough following the recipe on page 382.
Roll out the dough and place on an oiled baking sheet.
Cover and let rest for 25 minutes.
Place the potatoes in a saucepan of cold salted water and bring to a boil. Cook until tender. Drain, cool and peel.
Mash the potatoes with a potato ricer.
Spread the mashed potatoes over the pizza round.
Top with the tuna and sprinkle over the capers.
Season with a pinch of salt and drizzle with olive oil.
Bake for 20-25 minutes. Slice and serve hot.

⌐ For a vegetarian version, substitute the tuna with thinly sliced onions. For an extra-flavorful pizza, add small pieces of Gorgonzola cheese.

Preparation time **15 minutes**
Cooking time **25 minutes**
Level **easy**
Wine **Terlaner**

truffled pizza with sausage

Ingredients for 4 servings

Dough:

1½ tsps active dry yeast

3/4 cup plus 1 tbsp (200 ml) water

3¼ cups (14 oz or 400 g) all-purpose flour

4 tbsps extra-virgin olive oil

3 tsps salt

Topping:

3/4 cup (7 oz or 200 g) ready-made tomato sauce

9 oz (250 g) cow's milk mozzarella, thinly sliced

10½ oz (300 g) luganega sausage, thinly sliced

3 tsps truffle paste

4 tbsps extra-virgin olive oil, salt

◻ For a lighter flavor, substitute the truffle cream with thinly sliced, fresh porcini mushrooms sprinkled over the top of the pizza.

Dissolve the yeast in half of the water. Mound the flour on a work surface and make a well in the center. Add the yeast mixture to the well along with the remaining water, oil and salt. Mix to form a smooth dough. Transfer the dough to a floured mixing bowl, cover and let rise for 1 hour. Roll out the dough into a thin round and place it on an oiled baking sheet. Let rise for another 20 minutes.
Preheat the oven to 400°F (200°C or Gas Mark 6). Top the dough with a thin layer of tomato sauce, the mozzarella and the sausage. Mix the truffle paste with 3 tablespoons of olive oil and drizzle the mixture over the pizza. Sprinkle with a pinch of salt and bake for about 20 minutes.

Preparation time **20 minutes**
Cooking time **20 minutes**
Level **easy**
Beer **German Weizen**

shrimp, olive and arugula pizza

Ingredients for 4 servings

Dough:

1¾ tsps (12 g) active dry yeast
3/4 cup plus 1 tbsp (200 ml) warm water
salt, **1** tsp sugar
3 tbsps extra-virgin olive oil
3¼ cups (14 oz or 400 g) all-purpose flour

Topping:

10½ oz (300 g) mozzarella, sliced
1/2 cup (2 oz or 50 g) pitted black olives
10½ oz (300 g) button mushrooms, sliced
10½ oz (300 g) shrimp, shelled and deveined
2 tbsps extra-virgin olive oil
1 bunch of arugula, salt and pepper

Prepare the pizza dough following the recipe on page 382. Divide the dough into 4 balls, cover with a damp towel and let rise in a warm place.
Preheat the oven to 425°F (220°C or Gas Mark 7).
Roll out the pizza dough on a lightly floured work surface. Place the rounds on oiled baking sheets and top with the mozzarella, olives, mushrooms and shrimp.
Season with pinches of salt and pepper and drizzle with olive oil. Bake for 10 minutes. Remove from the oven, top with the arugula and serve immediately.

Preparation time **20 minutes**
Cooking time **15 minutes**
Level **easy**
Beer **Italian Lager**

truffled squash pizza

Ingredients for 4 servings

Dough:

1 ¾ tsps (12 g) active dry yeast
3/4 cup plus 1 tbsp (200 ml) warm water
salt, **1** tsp sugar
3 tbsps extra-virgin olive oil
3 ¼ cups (14 oz or 400 g) all-purpose flour

Topping:

1 lb (500 g) winter squash, peeled, deseeded and diced
7 tbsps heavy cream
4 tbsps grated Parmesan cheese, salt
freshly grated nutmeg
7 oz (200 g) mozzarella, diced
2 tbsps extra-virgin olive oil
1 black truffle

Prepare the pizza dough following the recipe on page 382.
Steam the squash until soft.
Puree together with the cream and Parmesan.
Season to taste with salt and nutmeg.
Preheat the oven to 400°F (200°C or Gas Mark 6).
Roll out the dough into 4 rounds, 1/5-inch (3 mm) thick, leaving a thick edge. Place the rounds on 4 oiled baking sheets. Spread the squash puree over the pizza rounds, top with mozzarella and drizzle with olive oil.
Bake for 20-25 minutes. Remove from the oven and slice the black truffle directly onto the pizzas using a truffle slicer. Serve immediately.

Preparation time **15 minutes**
Cooking time **40 minutes**
Level **easy**
Wine **Ribolla Gialla**

Special Pizzas

broccoli and anchovy pizza

Ingredients for 4 servings

Dough:

1¾ tsps (12 g) active dry yeast
3/4 cup plus 1 tbsp (200 ml) warm water
salt, **1** tsp sugar
3 tbsps extra-virgin olive oil
3¼ cups (14 oz or 400 g) all-purpose flour

Topping:

4¼ cups (10½ oz or 300 g) broccoli florets
3 tbsps chili-infused olive oil, salt
1 garlic clove, minced
6 anchovy fillets in salt, rinsed
1/2 cup (1½ oz or 40 g) pine nuts

Preheat the oven to 425°F (220°C or Gas Mark 7).
Prepare the pizza dough following the recipe on page 382.
Blanch the broccoli for 5 minutes in salted water.
Heat the chili oil in a large frying pan and add the garlic clove. When the garlic begins to brown add the anchovies and cook until they dissolve.
Stir a tablespoon of warm water to thin the sauce and add the blanched broccoli. Sauté for a few minutes, tossing the broccoli in the pan to coat it with the sauce.
Roll out the dough into a thin sheet and place it on an oiled baking sheet. Top with the broccoli sauce, sprinkle over the pine nuts and season with a pinch of salt.
Bake for about 30 minutes and serve immediately.

The anchovies may be substituted with sausage in this recipe. Brown the crumbled sausage in a frying pan with a little oil and then add the blanched broccoli.

Preparation time **20 minutes**
Cooking time **40 minutes**
Level **easy**
Beer **German Weizen**

baby octopus, olive and caper pizza

Ingredients for 4 servings

Dough:

1¾ tsps (12 g) active dry yeast

3/4 cup plus 1 tbsp (200 ml) warm water

salt, **1** tsp sugar

3 tbsps extra-virgin olive oil

3¼ cups (14 oz or 400 g) all-purpose flour

Topping:

4 tbsps extra-virgin olive oil

2 garlic cloves, oregano, salt

5½ oz (150 g) canned crushed tomatoes

14 oz (400 g) baby octopus

4 tbsps capers

2/3 cup (3½ oz or 100 g) pitted green olives, sliced

Whole unpeeled garlic cloves are called aglio in camicia in Italian, literally "garlic in a shirt." They are often used in Italian cooking to give a delicate garlic flavor that isn't overpowering.

Preheat the oven to 400°F (200°C or Gas Mark 6). Prepare the pizza dough following the recipe on page 382. Brown the whole, unpeeled garlic cloves in a frying pan with 2 tablespoons of olive oil. Add the crushed tomatoes and let cook for 8 minutes.
Season with salt and add the oregano.
Clean the baby octopus and let them soak in a bowl of ice water. Roll out the dough and place it on an oiled baking sheet. Spread over the tomato sauce and top with the olives, capers and baby octopus. Drizzle over a few tablespoons of olive oil and bake for 10 minutes.
Remove from the oven and serve immediately.

Preparation time **20 minutes**
Cooking time **20 minutes**
Level **easy**
Wine **Greco di Tufo**

Special Pizzas

pineapple and prosciutto pizza

Ingredients for 4 servings

Dough:

1¾ tsps (12 g) active dry yeast

3/4 cup plus 1 tbsp (200 ml) warm water

salt, **1** tsp sugar

3 tbsps extra-virgin olive oil

3¼ cups (14 oz or 400 g) all-purpose flour

Topping:

14 oz (400 g) mozzarella, diced

1 pineapple, peeled and cut into wedges

7 oz (200 g) prosciutto, thinly sliced

Preheat the oven to 400°F (200°C or Gas Mark 6). Prepare the pizza dough following the recipe on page 382. Place the mozzarella on a paper towel to dry out. Roll out the dough into 4 rounds and place on oiled baking sheets. Top with the mozzarella and bake for 8 minutes. Remove from the oven and top with the pineapple and the prosciutto. Serve immediately.

The pineapple may be substituted with fresh peeled and quartered figs.

Preparation time **25 minutes**
Cooking time **8 minutes**
Level **easy**
Wine **Prosecco di Conegliano e Valdobbiadene Extra Dry**

red pizza with bresaola and fennel

Ingredients for 4 servings

Dough:

1¾ tsps (12 g) active dry yeast

3/4 cup plus 1 tbsp (200 ml) warm water

salt, **1** tsp sugar

3 tbsps extra-virgin olive oil

3¼ cups (14 oz or 400 g) all-purpose flour

Topping:

2 fennel bulbs, trimmed and sliced into wedges

salt and pepper, oregano

7 oz (200 g) canned crushed tomatoes

4 tbsps extra-virgin olive oil

7 oz (200 g) bresaola, thinly sliced

Preheat the oven to 425°F (220°C or Gas Mark 7).
Prepare the pizza dough following the recipe on page 382.
Blanch the fennel in boiling salted water for 8 minutes.
Drain and let cool.
Puree the tomatoes and season with salt and pepper.
Roll out the dough into 4 rounds and place the rounds on oiled round baking sheets. Spread the tomato sauce on the pizzas and sprinkle over a pinch of oregano.
Top with the fennel wedges and drizzle with olive oil.
Bake for 20 minutes, remove from the oven and place the bresaola slices on the pizzas.
Serve immediately.

If desired, top this pizza with roughly chopped arugula when it comes out of the oven.

Preparation time **30 minutes**
Cooking time **30 minutes**
Level **easy**
Beer **Italian Pilsner**

carbonara pizza

Ingredients for 4 servings

Dough:

1¾ tsps (12 g) active dry yeast
3/4 cup plus 1 tbsp (200 ml) warm water
salt, **1** tsp sugar
3 tbsps extra-virgin olive oil
3¼ cups (14 oz or 400 g) all-purpose flour

Topping:

4 hard-boiled eggs
1/4 onion, minced , **4** tbsps minced parsley
2 tbsps extra-virgin olive oil
7 oz (200 g) canned crushed tomatoes
10½ oz (300 g) mozzarella, diced
7 oz (200 g) pancetta, diced

For a "white" version of this pizza, eliminate the tomato sauce and increase the quantity of mozzarella to 1 lb (450 g). Spread the diced cheese over the base of the pizzas and continue with the recipe.

Preheat the oven to 400°F (200°C or Gas Mark 6).
Prepare the pizza dough following the recipe on page 382.
Peel the eggs and smash them with a fork.
Sauté the onion in 2 tablespoons of olive oil.
Add the tomatoes and simmer for 10 minutes.
Puree the sauce or pass through a sieve.
Roll out the dough into 4 rounds and place them on oiled baking sheets. Spread the sauce on the pizzas using the back of a spoon and top with the mozzarella, pancetta and eggs. Bake for 15-20 minutes. Remove from the oven, sprinkle over the parsley and serve.

Preparation time **25 minutes**
Cooking time **25 minutes**
Level **easy**
Beer **Czech Pilsner**

ham and porcini pizza

Ingredients for 4 servings

Dough:

1¾ tsps (12 g) active dry yeast
3/4 cup plus 1 tbsp (200 ml) warm water
salt, **1** tsp sugar
3 tbsps extra-virgin olive oil
3¼ cups (14 oz or 400 g) all-purpose flour

Topping:

2 oz (50 g) dried porcini mushrooms
4 tbsps ready-made tomato sauce, salt
7 oz (200 g) mozzarella, sliced
4 large hot dogs, sliced
2 tbsps extra-virgin olive oil
7 oz (200 g) ham, thinly sliced

Preheat the oven to 400°F (200°C or Gas Mark 6). Prepare the pizza dough following the recipe on page 382. Soak the dried porcini in a little warm water for 10 minutes. Season the tomato sauce with a little salt. Roll out the pizza dough into 4 rounds and place them on oiled baking sheets. Spread 1 tablespoon of tomato sauce on each pizza. Top with the mozzarella, porcini mushrooms and hot dogs and drizzle with olive oil. Bake the pizzas for 20 minutes. Remove from the oven and top with the ham slices. Serve immediately.

If fresh porcini are available, use 9 oz (250 g) sliced fresh porcini mushrooms in place of the dried ones.

Preparation time **20 minutes**
Cooking time **20 minutes**
Level **easy**
Beer **German Pilsner**

savory pizza

Ingredients for 4 servings

Dough:

1¾ tsps (12 g) active dry yeast

¾ cup plus 1 tbsp (200 ml) warm water

salt, **1** tsp sugar

3 tbsps extra-virgin olive oil

3¼ cups (14 oz or 400 g) all-purpose flour

Topping:

2 tbsps extra-virgin olive oil

7 oz (200 g) canned crushed tomatoes

10½ oz (300 g) mozzarella, diced

4 mild Italian sausages, sliced

3½ oz (100 g) semi-aged truffled cheese, shaved

2 small black truffles, salt

If truffled cheese is unavailable, use a semi-aged Tuscan pecorino instead.

Preheat the oven to 400°F (200°C or Gas Mark 6). Prepare the pizza dough following the recipe on page 382. Heat 2 tablespoons of olive oil in a frying pan and add the crushed tomatoes. Simmer for 10 minutes and season to taste with salt.

Roll out the pizza dough into 4 thin rounds. Place the dough on oiled baking sheets and spread the tomato sauce onto the pizzas. Top with the mozzarella, sausage and truffled cheese.

Bake for 20 minutes. Remove the pizzas from the oven and top with the shaved black truffles. Serve immediately.

Preparation time **30 minutes**
Cooking time **20 minutes**
Level **easy**
Beer **German Weizen**

pizza with tuna and zucchini flowers

Ingredients for 4 servings

Dough:

1¾ tsps (12 g) active dry yeast

3/4 cup plus 1 tbsp (200 ml) warm water

salt, **1** tsp sugar

3 tbsps extra-virgin olive oil

3¼ cups (14 oz or 400 g) all-purpose flour

Topping:

4 small zucchini with flowers attached

4 tbsps extra-virgin olive oil, sugar

2 garlic cloves, salt and pepper

7 oz (200 g) canned crushed tomatoes

10½ oz (300 g) tuna in oil, drained and crumbled

10½ oz (300 g) mozzarella, diced

⌐ Try substituting the sautéed zucchini with julienned strips of red and yellow bell pepper.

Preheat the oven to 400°F (200°C or Gas Mark 6). Prepare the pizza dough following the recipe on page 382. Slice the zucchini and open the flowers, removing the pistils. Sauté the zucchini in a frying pan with 2 tablespoons of olive oil and the garlic cloves. Season to taste with salt and set aside.
Puree the tomatoes with 2 tablespoons of olive oil and pinches of salt, pepper and sugar. Roll out the dough and place it on 4 oiled baking sheets. Spread a thin layer of tomato sauce over each pizza and top with the mozzarella, sautéed zucchini, tuna and zucchini flowers. Bake for 20 minutes and serve very hot.

Preparation time **30 minutes**
Cooking time **20 minutes**
Level **easy**
Wine **Bianco d'Alcamo Riserva**

Special Pizzas

zighini pizza

Ingredients for 4 servings

Dough:

1¾ tsps (12 g) active dry yeast
3/4 cup plus 1 tbsp (200 ml) warm water
salt, **1** tsp sugar
3 tbsps extra-virgin olive oil
3¼ cups (14 oz or 400 g) all-purpose flour

Topping:

4 tbsps extra-virgin olive oil
1¼ cups (5½ oz or 150 g) finely diced onion, carrot and celery
10½ oz (300 g) ground beef and pork
1/2 cup (120 ml) red wine
14 oz (400 g) canned crushed tomatoes
2 dried red chili peppers, salt and pepper
10½ oz (300 g) mozzarella, diced

Prepare the pizza dough following the recipe on page 382. Heat 2 tablespoons of olive oil in a large frying pan and add the onion, carrot and celery mixture. Sauté until soft then add the ground meat, breaking it up with the back of a spoon. Brown the meat and then add the red wine. Let evaporate and add two-thirds of the tomatoes. Crumble in the dried chili peppers, season to taste with salt and pepper and cook for 30 minutes.
Preheat the oven to 425°F (220°C or Gas Mark 7). Roll out the pizza dough into 4 rounds and place them on oiled baking sheets.
Spread a thin layer of the remaining crushed tomatoes over each pizza. Top with the mozzarella and the meat sauce. Bake for 10 minutes and serve immediately.

Browning ingredients means to cook them until a golden-brown crust forms on the surface.

Preparation time **20 minutes**
Cooking time **40 minutes**
Level **easy**
Beer **German Weizen**

vegetarian pizzas

calabrian pizza with capers and eggplant

Ingredients for 4 servings

Dough:
11 oz (300 g) pizza dough (see page 382)

Topping:
1 eggplant, sliced
1¼ cups (10 oz or 280 g) diced buffalo's milk mozzarella
1 tbsp capers, drained and rinsed
20 cherry tomatoes, quartered
3 tbsps extra-virgin olive oil
salt and pepper
fresh basil leaves, torn

Preheat oven to 450°F (230°C). Divide the pizza dough into 4 balls. Cover the dough with a damp cloth and let rise. Heat a cast-iron grill pan and grill the eggplant slices for 2 minutes on each side.
Roll the dough balls out into thin rounds. Place the pizza bases on an oiled baking sheet or hot pizza stone. Sprinkle with mozzarella, capers and tomatoes and season with olive oil, salt and pepper. Bake for 8 minutes.
Add the eggplant slices to the top of the pizza and continue baking until the edges are browned and crispy. Remove from the oven, sprinkle with basil and serve immediately.

⌐ For a thicker pizza, roll out the dough in an oiled baking tray, sprinkle with tomatoes, capers and mozzarella cheese and leave to rise in a warm place. Bake in a preheated 425°F (220°C or Gas Mark 7) oven for 12 minutes, adding the eggplant after 6 minutes.

Preparation time **20 minutes**
Cooking time **15 minutes**
Level **easy**
Beer **Italian Lager**

autumn pizza

Ingredients for 4 servings

Dough:

1¾ tsps (12 g) active dry yeast

3/4 cup plus 1 tbsp (200 ml) warm water

salt, **1** tsp sugar

3 tbsps extra-virgin olive oil

3¼ cups (14 oz or 400 g) all-purpose flour

Topping:

2 tbsps (1 oz or 30 g) butter

1/4 cup (1 oz or 30 g) all-purpose flour

3/4 cup plus 1 tbsp (200 ml) cold milk

7 oz (200 g) fontina cheese, diced

14 oz (400 g) fresh porcini mushrooms

4 tbsps extra-virgin olive oil

salt

1 tbsp minced parsley

7 oz (200 g) mozzarella, diced

Prepare the pizza dough following the recipe on page 382. Preheat the oven to 400°F (200°C or Gas Mark 6).
Melt the butter in a saucepan and add the flour. Cook for 2 minutes, stirring constantly. Whisk in the cold milk, and continue to stir to prevent lumps from forming. When the sauce begins to thicken add the fontina cheese and remove from heat. Continue stirring until the cheese has melted completely, then set aside.
Cut off the earthy part of the mushroom stalks and clean the caps with a damp paper towel. Thinly slice the mushrooms and sauté with 2 tablespoons of olive oil for a few minutes. Season with a pinch of salt and sprinkle with parsley. Roll out the dough on a lightly floured surface into 4 thin discs, about 1/5-inch (3 mm) thick, leaving a thicker border around the edge. Place the rounds on lightly oiled baking sheets. Spread a few tablespoons of the fontina sauce over the pizzas and top with the mozzarella and sautéed mushrooms. Bake for 25 minutes.
Remove the pizzas from the oven and serve immediately.

Preparation time **20 minutes**
Cooking time **40 minutes**
Level **easy**
Beer **Irish Stout**

mushroom and arugula pizza

vegetarian pizzas

Ingredients for 4 servings

Dough:

1¾ tsps (12 g) active dry yeast

3/4 cup plus 1 tbsp (200 ml) warm water

salt, **1** tsp sugar

3 tbsps extra-virgin olive oil

3¼ cups (14 oz or 400 g) all-purpose flour

Topping:

3/4 cup plus 1 tbsp (200 ml) ready-made tomato sauce

3⅓ cups (9 oz or 250 g) thinly sliced button mushrooms

3 tbsps extra-virgin olive oil, parsley

2 bunches (about 4 oz or 120 g) arugula, coarsely chopped

7 oz (200 g) ricotta salata (see note), shaved

salt and pepper

If ricotta salata is unavailable, use provolone, Parmesan or Pecorino.

Prepare the pizza dough following the recipe on page 382. Preheat the oven to 400°F (200°C or Gas Mark 6). Roll out the dough on a lightly floured surface into 4 thin circles, about 9 inches (22 cm) in diameter and 1/5-inch (3 mm) thick. Place the rounds on lightly oiled baking sheets. Spread a layer of tomato sauce over each pizza and bake for 10 minutes.
Place the mushrooms in a bowl, season with pinches of salt and pepper and drizzle with 3 tablespoons of olive oil. Add the parsley and carefully mix to combine.
Top the hot pizzas with the mushrooms, arugula and ricotta salata shavings. Drizzle over more olive oil if desired.

Preparation time **15 minutes**
Cooking time **10 minutes**
Level **easy**
Beer **Pilsner**

bell pepper and smoked scamorza pizza

Ingredients for 4 servings

Dough:

1¾ tsps (12 g) active dry yeast

3/4 cup plus 1 tbsp (200 ml) warm water

salt, **1** tsp sugar

3 tbsps extra-virgin olive oil

3¼ cups (14 oz or 400 g) all-purpose flour

Topping:

2 red bell peppers, deseeded and sliced

1 yellow bell pepper, deseeded and sliced

5 tbsps extra-virgin olive oil, salt

7 oz (200 g) smoked scamorza, diced

3¼ oz (150 g) buffalo mozzarella, diced

2/3 cup (150 ml) ready-made tomato sauce

Prepare the pizza dough following the recipe on page 382.
Sauté the bell peppers in 2 tablespoons of olive oil until they are soft. Season with salt and set aside.
Mix together the scamorza and mozzarella.
Preheat the oven to 400°F (200°C or Gas Mark 6).
Spread the dough into an oiled rectangular baking sheet using the fingertips. Drizzle with 1 tablespoon of olive oil and let rise for 25 minutes.
Spread a thin layer of tomato sauce over the pizza.
Top with the sautéed peppers and cheese mixture. Drizzle over the remaining olive oil and bake for 10-15 minutes.

Preparation time **15 minutes**
Cooking time **25 minutes**
Level **easy**
Beer **German Weizen**

white pizza with truffle oil

vegetarian pizzas

Ingredients for 4 servings
Dough:
1¾ tsps (12 g) active dry yeast
3/4 cup plus 1 tbsp (200 ml) warm water
salt, **1** tsp sugar
3 tbsps extra-virgin olive oil
3¼ cups (14 oz or 400 g) all-purpose flour
Topping:
2 fresh porcini mushrooms
3 tbsps truffle oil, salt
9 oz (250 g) mozzarella, diced
5 oz (150 g) Parmesan, shaved

Prepare the pizza dough following the recipe on page 382. Preheat oven to 450°F (230°C or Gas Mark 8).
Cut off the earthy part of the mushroom stalk and wipe the mushrooms clean with a damp paper towel.
Cut the mushrooms in half lengthwise then slice them. Divide the dough into 4 portions and roll them out into rounds. Place on 4 oiled baking sheets, drizzle with truffle oil and season with salt. Top with the mozzarella and porcini. Sprinkle over the Parmesan, then bake for 8 minutes or until the crust is cooked through.
Serve immediately.

⌐ If fresh porcini mushrooms are not available, use porcini preserved in olive oil, making sure to drain them well before placing them on the pizzas.

Preparation time **10 minutes**
Cooking time **10 minutes**
Level **easy**
Beer **English Pale Ale**

lucana pizza with pecorino and basil

vegetarian pizzas

Ingredients for 4 servings

Dough:

1¾ tsps (12 g) active dry yeast

3/4 cup plus 1 tbsp (200 ml) warm water

salt, **1** tsp sugar

3 tbsps extra-virgin olive oil

3¼ cups (14 oz or 400 g) all-purpose flour

Topping:

14 oz (400 g) canned crushed tomatoes

8½ oz (240 g) pecorino, diced

1 bunch fresh basil, 1/2 whole and 1/2 chiffonaded

3 tbsps extra-virgin olive oil, salt

Prepare the pizza dough following the recipe on page 382. Preheat the oven to 450°F (230°C or Gas Mark 8). Spread the dough into 4 oiled rectangular baking sheets using the fingertips. Spread a thin layer of the crushed tomatoes over the pizzas, leaving an empty border around the edges. Season with pinches of salt and top with the pecorino. Drizzle with 3 tablespoons of olive oil and bake for 20 minutes.
Remove the pizzas from the oven and top with the basil leaves and basil chiffonade. Serve immediately.

⌐ While many types of pecorino cheese are available, for this recipe it is best to use a mild, fresh variety.

Preparation time **20 minutes**
Cooking time **20 minutes**
Level **easy**
Beer **Italian Lager**

pizza with smoked provola and asparagus

Ingredients for 4 servings

Dough:

1½ tsps active dry yeast

1 cup minus 1 tbsp (220 ml) water

3⅔ cups (1 lb or 450 g) all-purpose flour

4 tbsps extra-virgin olive oil

3 tsps salt

Topping:

14 oz (400 g) asparagus

9 oz (250 g) cow's milk mozzarella, sliced

10½ oz (300 g) smoked provola or other mild smoked cheese, diced

3 tbsps extra-virgin olive oil

salt and pepper

Dissolve the yeast in half of the water. Mound the flour on a work surface and make a well in the center.
Pour the yeast mixture into the well and add the remaining water, oil and salt. Mix to form a dough and knead until smooth and elastic. Roll the dough into a ball and place in a floured bowl. Cover and let rise at room temperature for 1 hour 30 minutes.
Meanwhile, trim the tough woody ends off the asparagus stalks and slice the stems into rounds, leaving the tips intact. Blanch the asparagus for 1 minute in boiling salted water, drain and set aside.
Preheat the oven to 400°F (200°C or Gas Mark 6).
Mix together the cheeses.
Divide the dough in half and roll out each half into a thin round. Place the dough rounds on oiled baking sheets. Top the pizzas with the cheeses and the asparagus. Drizzle with olive oil and sprinkle with pinches of salt and pepper. Bake for about 20 minutes, slice and serve hot.

Preparation time **20 minutes**
Cooking time **20 minutes**
Level **easy**
Beer **Italian Lager**

vegetarian pizzas

pizza with walnuts and brie

Ingredients for 4 servings

Dough:

1½ tsps active dry yeast

1 cup minus 1 tbsp (220 ml) water

3⅔ cups (1 lb or 450 g) all-purpose flour

4 tbsps extra-virgin olive oil

3 tsps salt

Topping:

9 oz (250 g) cow's milk mozzarella, sliced

14 oz (400 g) Brie cheese

3/4 cup (3 oz or 80 g) walnut halves

extra-virgin olive oil

salt and pepper

2 bunches of basil, torn

Dissolve the yeast in half of the water. Sift the flour onto a work surface and make a well in the center. Pour the yeast mixture into the well and add the remaining water, the olive oil and a pinch of salt.
Mix to form a dough and knead until smooth and elastic. Roll the dough into a ball and place in a floured bowl. Cover and let rise at room temperature for 1 hour.
Preheat the oven to 400°F (200°C or Gas Mark 6).
On a lightly floured surface, roll out the dough into 4 rounds. Place the rounds on a lightly oiled baking sheet. Lay the mozzarella slices on a paper towel to absorb excess moisture. Break up the Brie into small pieces. Top the pizzas with the cheeses and the walnut halves. Drizzle with olive oil and sprinkle with a pinch of salt and freshly ground pepper. Bake for 20 minutes. Top with the torn basil leaves before serving.

Preparation time **25 minutes**
Cooking time **20 minutes**
Level **easy**
Beer **Belgium White**

vegetarian pizzas

buffalo mozzarella pizza with green olive tapenade

vegetarian pizzas

Ingredients for 4 servings
Dough:
1½ tsps active dry yeast
1 cup minus 1 tbsp (220 ml) water
3⅔ cups (1 lb or 450 g) all-purpose flour
4 tbsps extra-virgin olive oil
3 tsps salt
Topping:
1 lb (500 g) buffalo mozzarella, diced
7 oz (200 g) cherry tomatoes, halved
7 oz (200 g) green olive tapenade
extra-virgin olive oil, salt
1 bunch of basil

Dissolve the yeast in half of the water. Mound the flour on a work surface and make a well in the center.
Pour the yeast mixture into the well and add the remaining water, olive oil and salt. Mix to form a dough and knead until smooth and elastic. Roll the dough into a ball and place in a floured bowl. Cover and let rise at room temperature for 1 hour 30 minutes.
Preheat the oven to 400°F (200°C or Gas Mark 6).
Divide the dough into quarters and roll out each quarter into a thin round. Place the pizza rounds on an oiled baking sheet.
Lay the mozzarella on a paper towel to absorb any excess moisture. Top the pizzas with the cheese, tomatoes and spoonfuls of tapenade. Drizzle with olive oil and sprinkle with salt and the torn basil leaves.
Bake for about 20 minutes and serve hot.

Green olive tapenade can be bought or made at home. Blend 7 oz (200 g) pitted green olives with 4 tablespoons extra-virgin olive oil and season to taste with salt.

Preparation time **25 minutes**
Cooking time **20 minutes**
Level **easy**
Beer **Belgium White**

arugula and fresh cheese pizza

Ingredients for 4 servings

Dough:

1¾ tsps (12 g) active dry yeast

3/4 cup plus 1 tbsp (200 ml) warm water

salt, **1** tsp sugar

3 tbsps extra-virgin olive oil

3¼ cups (14 oz or 400 g) all-purpose flour

Topping:

3½ oz (100 g) mozzarella, diced

salt and pepper

2 bunches arugula, coarsely chopped

7 oz (200 g) soft, fresh, spreadable cheese

4 tbsps extra-virgin olive oil

Prepare the pizza dough following the recipe on page 382. Preheat the oven to 425°F (220°C or Gas Mark 7). Squeeze any excess water out of the mozzarella and set aside. Roll out the dough into 4 rounds on a lightly floured work surface. Place the rounds on 4 oiled baking sheets. Pierce the base of the pizzas with a fork and top with the mozzarella. Season with pinches of salt and freshly ground pepper. Bake for 20 minutes, remove the pizzas from the oven and top with the arugula and fresh cheese. Drizzle with olive oil and serve immediately.

For more flavor and a colorful addition, add 7 oz (200 g) of cherry tomatoes to the pizza before serving.

Preparation time **20 minutes**
Cooking time **20 minutes**
Level **easy**
Beer **German Weizen**

vegetable and mozzarella pizza

Ingredients for 4 servings

Dough:
2½ tsps (20 g) active dry yeast
1/2 cup (120 ml) warm water
1⅔ cups (7 oz or 200 g) whole-wheat flour
1⅔ cups (7 oz or 200 g) all-purpose flour
2 tbsps extra-virgin olive oil, salt

Topping:
4 carrots, julienned, 4 tsps oregano
2 yellow bell peppers, julienned
4 small zucchini, julienned
4 tbsps ready-made tomato sauce
2 whole buffalo mozzarellas, diced
4 tbsps extra-virgin olive oil

Dissolve the yeast in the warm water. Mix together the different flours and add the yeast mixture. Add the salt, olive oil and enough water to form a thick dough. Knead until smooth and elastic, cover with a clean kitchen towel and let rise for 2 hours.
Preheat the oven to 350°F (180°C or Gas Mark 4).
Sauté the carrots, bell peppers and zucchini in the olive oil for 5 minutes.
Spread the dough into an oiled rectangular baking sheet and spread over a thin layer of tomato sauce.
Top with the sautéed vegetables, sprinkle with oregano and bake for 20 minutes. Remove from the oven, top the pizza with the mozzarella and bake for another 10 minutes.

Mozzarella made from buffalo's milk *(mozzarella di bufala)* is typical of the southern Italian region of Campania. It has a moisture content and a delicate flavor, and should be eaten as fresh as possible.

Preparation time **15 minutes**
Cooking time **35 minutes**
Level **easy**
Beer **Belgian White**

spicy onion and olive pizza

Ingredients for 4 servings

Dough:

1¾ tsps (12 g) active dry yeast
3/4 cup plus 1 tbsp (200 ml) warm water
salt, **1** tsp sugar
3 tbsps extra-virgin olive oil
3¼ cups (14 oz or 400 g) all-purpose flour

Topping:

4 onions, thinly sliced
5 tbsps extra-virgin olive oil, salt
3/4 cup plus 1 tbsp (200 ml) ready-made tomato sauce
ground chili pepper, oregano
12½ oz (350 g) mozzarella, diced
5 tbsps (2 oz or 50 g) pitted black olives

Prepare the pizza dough following the recipe on page 382. Preheat the oven to 400°F (200°C or Gas Mark 6).
Rinse the onions under cold running water, drain and place in a bowl. Dress the onions with 3 tablespoons olive oil and a pinch of salt.
Roll out the dough into 4 thin rounds on a lightly floured work surface. Place each pizza on an oiled baking sheet. Add the ground chili pepper and a pinch of salt to the tomato sauce and mix well.
Spread a thin layer of tomato sauce over each pizza and top with the mozzarella, onions and black olives. Drizzle with olive oil and bake for 20-25 minutes.

Preparation time **15 minutes**
Cooking time **25 minutes**
Level **easy**
Beer **Italian Lager**

pizza with sweet corn, arugula and parmesan

Ingredients for 4 servings
Dough:
1½ tsps active dry yeast
1 cup minus 1 tbsp (220 ml) water
3⅔ cups (1 lb or 450 g) all-purpose flour
4 tbsps extra-virgin olive oil, 3 tsps salt

Topping:
1 cup (9 oz or 250 g) ready-made tomato sauce
12½ oz (350 g) cow's milk mozzarella, diced
3/4 cups (6½ oz or 180 g) canned or frozen sweet corn
extra-virgin olive oil, salt
5½ oz (150 g) Parmesan cheese, shaved
1 bunch (4 oz or 120 g) arugula

For a savory, low-fat variation, substitute the corn with bresaola. This delicious air-dried beef is low in fat and calories.

Dissolve the yeast in half of the water. Sift the flour onto a work surface and make a well in the center.
Pour the yeast mixture into the well and add the remaining water, olive oil and salt.
Mix to form a dough and knead until smooth and elastic. Roll the dough into a ball and place in a floured bowl. Cover and let rise at room temperature for 1 hour 30 minutes.
Preheat the oven to 400°F (200°C or Gas Mark 6).
Divide the dough into quarters and roll out each one into a thin round on a lightly floured surface, then transfer to an oiled baking sheet.
Top each pizza with a layer of tomato sauce and sprinkle over the mozzarella and sweet corn.
Drizzle with olive oil and season with a pinch of salt
Bake for about 20 minutes, remove from the oven and top with the arugula and Parmesan shavings. Serve hot.

Preparation time **25 minutes**
Cooking time **20 minutes**
Level **easy**
Beer **German Weizen**

olive pizza with fresh tomatoes

Ingredients for 4 servings
Dough:
1¾ tsps (12 g) active dry yeast
3/4 cup plus 1 tbsp (200 ml) warm water
salt, **1** tsp sugar
3 tbsps extra-virgin olive oil
3¼ cups (14 oz or 400 g) all-purpose flour
Topping:
5½ oz (150 g) canned crushed tomatoes
4 tbsps extra-virgin olive oil, salt
4 ripe tomatoes, thinly sliced
7 oz (200 g) buffalo mozzarella, chopped
1 cup (120 g) black and green olives

Prepare the pizza dough following the recipe on page 382. Preheat the oven to 400°F (200°C or Gas Mark 6).
Roll out the dough into a 1/2-inch (1 cm) thick rectangle and place on an oiled baking sheet.
Cover and let rise for 25-30 minutes.
Puree the crushed tomatoes with a pinch of salt and 2 tablespoons of olive oil. Spread a thin layer of tomato sauce over the pizza. Cover the pizza with the tomato slices. Drain the mozzarella in a colander and place it in a mixing bowl. Season with pinches of salt and pepper and drizzle with olive oil. Distribute the mozzarella evenly over the pizza. Sprinkle the olives over the pizza and bake for 15-20 minutes. Remove from the oven, cut into rectangles and serve immediately.

vegetarian pizzas

For an aromatic touch, top the cooked pizza with fresh basil or oregano.

Preparation time **10 minutes**
Cooking time **20 minutes**
Level **easy**
Wine **Cirò Bianco**

pizza with fontina, ricotta and cherry tomatoes

Ingredients for 4 servings
Dough:

3¼ tsps active dry yeast
7 tbsps warm water
2 lbs (1 kg) bread flour
salt and pepper
1/2 cup (3½ oz or 100 g) lard
1½ cups (5½ oz 150 g) grated Parmesan cheese
2½ oz (75 g) ricotta
13 eggs
3 egg yolks
1 lb (500 g) sliced fontina cheese
20 cherry tomatoes, halved
3 tbsps extra-virgin olive oil

Dissolve the yeast in the warm water. Mix together the flour, yeast mixture, salt, lard, Parmesan and ricotta. Beat the eggs and egg yolks together and add them to the dough. Knead until smooth and elastic.
Cover the dough with a clean kitchen towel and let rise until doubled in volume.
Preheat the oven to 400°F (200°C or Gas Mark 6).
Lightly oil 2 small baking sheets or 1 large baking sheet.
Push the dough over the baking sheet, using the fingertips, until covered completely.
Bake for 10 minutes, remove from the oven, top with the tomatoes and fontina and drizzle with olive oil.
Return to the oven and bake for another 10 minutes.
Top with freshly ground pepper and serve the pizza hot.

Preparation time **10 minutes**
Cooking time **20 minutes**
Level **easy**
Beer **Pilsner**

white pizza with asparagus and cherry tomatoes

Ingredients for 4 servings

Dough:

1¾ tsps (12 g) active dry yeast

3/4 cup plus 1 tbsp (200 ml) warm water

salt, **1** tsp sugar

3 tbsps extra-virgin olive oil

3¼ cups (14 oz or 400 g) all-purpose flour

Topping:

14 oz (400 g) asparagus, trimmed

10½ oz (300 g) mozzarella, diced

7 oz (200 g) cherry tomatoes, quartered

3 tbsps extra-virgin olive oil, salt

Prepare the pizza dough following the recipe on page 382.
Spread the pizza dough onto 2 well-oiled baking sheets.
Cover and let rise for 30 minutes.
Preheat the oven to 400°F (200°C or Gas Mark 6).
Boil the asparagus spears for 10 minutes in lightly salted water. Drain and cool in a bowl of ice water.
Chop the chilled asparagus into rounds.
Top the pizza with the mozzarella, asparagus and cherry tomatoes and season with a pinch of salt. Drizzle with 2 tablespoons of olive oil and bake for 15 minutes.
Remove from the oven, and serve immediately.

If desired, top the cooked pizza with Parmesan cheese shavings.

Preparation time **20 minutes**
Cooking time **25 minutes**
Level **easy**
Wine **Sicilia Chardonnay**

endive and brie pizza

Ingredients for 4 servings

Dough:

1¾ tsps (12 g) active dry yeast
3/4 cup plus 1 tbsp (200 ml) warm water
salt, **1** tsp sugar
3 tbsps extra-virgin olive oil
3¼ cups (14 oz or 400 g) all-purpose flour

Topping:

14 oz (400 g) Brie cheese, diced
salt
9 oz (250 g) endive, thinly sliced
4 tbsps extra-virgin olive oil

Prepare the pizza dough following the recipe on page 382. Preheat the oven to 400°F (200°C or Gas Mark 6). Roll out the dough into 4 small rounds and place the rounds on 4 small oiled baking sheets. Top the pizzas with the Brie, leaving an empty border around the edges.
Season the pizzas with salt and sprinkle over the endive, reserving a handful for garnish. Drizzle with the olive oil and bake for 15 minutes. Remove the pizzas from the oven, add the remaining endive and drizzle with olive oil if desired.

Brie may be substituted with the same quantity of Gorgonzola, Asiago, or fontina cheese and the endive may be replaced with radicchio.

Preparation time **20 minutes**
Cooking time **15 minutes**
Level **easy**
Beer **Italian Lager**

pizza with onions and cannellini beans

Ingredients for 4 servings

Dough:

1¾ tsps (12 g) active dry yeast
3/4 cup plus 1 tbsp (200 ml) warm water
salt, **1** tsp sugar
3 tbsps extra-virgin olive oil
3¼ cups (14 oz or 400 g) all-purpose flour

Topping:

3/4 cup (5½ oz or 150 g) dried cannellini beans, soaked overnight
7 oz (200 g) canned crushed tomatoes
9 oz (250 g) mozzarella, diced
2 onions, thinly sliced, salt and pepper
4 tbsps extra-virgin olive oil

Prepare the pizza dough following the recipe on page 382. Divide the dough into 4 parts and let rise. Boil the beans in salted water for 50 minutes. Drain and set aside. Soak the onions in ice water for 10 minutes. Drain and set aside. Pass the tomatoes through a sieve and season them with pinches of salt and pepper. Preheat the oven to 425°F (200°C or Gas Mark 7). Roll out the pizza into 4 rounds and place them on oiled baking sheets. Spread the tomato sauce over the pizzas using the back of a spoon. Top with the mozzarella, cannellini beans and onions.
Drizzle with olive oil and bake for 10 minutes. Serve immediately.

⌐ This pizza may be enriched by adding 7 oz (200 g) tuna in olive oil, drained and crumbled.

Preparation time **15 minutes**
Cooking time **1 hour**
Level **easy**
Beer **English Ale**

vegetarian pizzas

pizza with french fries

Ingredients for 4 servings

Dough:

1¾ tsps (12 g) active dry yeast

3/4 cup plus 1 tbsp (200 ml) warm water

salt, **1** tsp sugar

3 tbsps extra-virgin olive oil

3¼ cups (14 oz or 400 g) all-purpose flour

Topping:

1 large white-fleshed potato (about 10½ oz or 300 g)

sunflower oil, salt, **1** tsp sugar

7 oz (200 g) canned crushed tomatoes

10½ oz (300 g) mozzarella, diced

Prepare the pizza dough following the recipe on page 382. Peel the potato and cut it into strips. Soak in ice water for 10 minutes to eliminate the starch. Drain and spread the potato strips onto paper towels to dry.
Heat abundant sunflower oil in a large saucepan and fry the potato strips until golden. Drain and let dry on paper towels.
Preheat the oven to 400°F (200°C or Gas Mark 6). Puree or sieve the crushed tomatoes. Cook in a small saucepan for 5 minutes. Add sugar, season to taste with salt and cook for another 5 minutes.
Roll out the dough into 4 rounds and place them on oiled baking sheets. Spread the tomato sauce over the pizzas and top with the mozzarella. Bake for 10 minutes. Remove from heat and top with the French fries. Season the pizzas with salt and serve immediately.

For a lighter version, thinly slice the potatoes, season with salt, rosemary and olive oil and bake for 15 minutes. Top the unbaked pizzas with the potatoes and proceed with the recipe.

Preparation time **30 minutes**
Cooking time **25 minutes**
Level **easy**
Beer **German Weizen**

focaccias

Pizza

liguria-style focaccia

Ingredients for 6 servings
Dough:

1¾ tsps (12 g) active dry yeast

3/4 cup plus 1 tbsp (200 ml) warm water

salt, **1** tsp sugar

4 tbsps extra-virgin olive oil

3¼ cups (14 oz or 400 g) all-purpose flour

coarse sea salt

In a large mixing bowl, dissolve the yeast in 1 cup plus 1 tablespoon (260 ml) water and add the sugar. Let sit for 5-10 minutes. Add the flour and 1 teaspoon salt and knead to form a smooth and soft dough. Do not work the dough for very long. Oil a baking sheet and then spread the dough over the sheet, using lightly oiled hands and fingertips. Let rest in a warm place for about 1 hour. Preheat the oven to 425°F (220°C or Gas Mark 7). Oil the hands and, using the fingertips, make a series of evenly spaced indentations in the dough. Sprinkle sea salt in the indentations. Bake for 10 minutes. Meanwhile, whisk together 3 tablespoons water and 2 tablespoons olive oil. Remove the focaccia from the oven and drizzle the emulsion over the focaccia. Return to the oven and bake for another 5-10 minutes, until golden-brown.
Serve the focaccia warm, sliced into strips.

Preparation time **20 minutes**
Cooking time **40 minutes**
Level **easy**
Wine **Torbato di Alghero**

stuffed focaccia with ricotta and nettles

Ingredients for 6 servings

Dough:

2½ (20 g) tsps active dry yeast

1¼ cups (300 ml) water, butter

4 cups (1 lb 1½ oz or 500 g) all-purpose flour

2 tbsps extra-virgin olive oil, salt

Topping:

10½ oz (300 g) nettles (see note)

4 tbsps extra-virgin olive oil

1 garlic clove, smashed

9 oz (250 g) ricotta

salt and pepper

coarse sea salt

Prepare the dough following the recipe on page 384. Blanch the nettles in boiling salted water for 5 minutes. Coarsely chop the blanched nettles and sauté them with 1 tablespoon of olive oil and the smashed garlic clove. Transfer to a mixing bowl and add the ricotta. Season to taste with salt and pepper. Divide the dough in half and roll it out into 2 rounds. Line an oiled round cake pan with one dough round. Top with the ricotta mixture and cover with the second dough round. Let rise for 30 minutes. Preheat the oven to 375°F (190°C or Gas Mark 5). Brush the top of the focaccia with olive oil and sprinkle with the coarse sea salt. Bake for 25-30 minutes. Serve the focaccia hot or warm, as desired.

Instead of nettles, this recipe could be prepared with a mix of burdock and nettles, or which fresh spinach and an aromatic herb of choice.

Preparation time **30 minutes**
Cooking time **35 minutes**
Level **easy**
Wine **Prosecco di Conegliano e Valdobbiadene Brut**

focaccia with anchovies and zucchini flowers

Ingredients for 6 servings

Dough:

2½ tsps active dry yeast
1¼ cups (300 ml) warm water
4 cups (1 lb 1½ oz or 500 g) all-purpose flour
1 tbsp salt
extra-virgin olive oil
2½ oz (70 g) anchovy fillets in oil, chopped
10 zucchini flowers, thinly sliced

Dissolve the yeast in a little warm water. Mix together the flour, yeast mixture, salt and remaining water to form a smooth dough. Place in a bowl and brush with olive oil. Cover and let rest for 30 minutes.
Preheat the oven to 400°F (200°C or Gas Mark 6). Add the anchovies and zucchini flowers and knead to evenly incorporate the ingredients.
Push the dough out onto an oiled baking sheet into a layer 1/2-inch (1 cm) thick. Let rest for 20 minutes. Using the fingertips, make small indentations on the surface of the focaccia. Season with a pinch of salt and bake for about 20 minutes. Let cool slightly and serve.

Try adding a few quartered cherry tomatoes to the topping sauce.

Preparation time **20 minutes**
Cooking time **20 minutes**
Level **easy**
Wine **Prosecco di Conegliano Brut**

potato focaccia with gorgonzola and marjoram

Ingredients for 6 servings

Dough:

2½ tsps active dry yeast

1 cup (250 ml) water

4 cups (1 lb 1½ oz or 500 g) all-purpose flour

1½ cups (10½ oz or 300 g) mashed potatoes

extra-virgin olive oil

14 oz (400 g) Gorgonzola cheese, diced

marjoram

salt and pepper

Dissolve the yeast in the water.
Mix together the flour and mashed potatoes then add the yeast mixture and salt. Knead to form a smooth dough and place in an oiled mixing bowl. Cover with a clean kitchen towel and let rest for 30 minutes.
Preheat the oven to 425°F (220°C or Gas Mark 7).
Roll out the dough into a layer 3/4-inch (1½ cm) thick and place it on an oiled baking sheet.
Let rise for 20 minutes and then make indentations over the surface of the dough using the fingertips.
Top with the pieces of Gorgonzola. Drizzle with olive oil and season with pepper and marjoram.
Bake for 10 minutes, then lower the oven temperature to 350°F (180°C or Gas Mark 4) and continue baking until cooked through.

For a smoother flavor, substitute the Gorgonzola with a milder cheese like mozzarella and add thinly sliced prosciutto or ham.

Preparation time **15 minutes**
Cooking time **20 minutes**
Level **easy**
Wine **Orvieto Classico**

potato focaccia with rosemary

Ingredients for 8 servings

Dough:

1 large potato

salt and pepper

5 tsps active dry yeast

1 cup (250 ml) water

3/4 cup plus 1 tbsp (200 ml) extra-virgin olive oil

4 cups (1 lb 1½ oz or 500 g) all-purpose flour

1 rosemary sprig, leaves only

coarse salt

Boil the potato in salted water until soft. Peel and mash. Dissolve the yeast in the water and half of the olive oil. Add pinches of salt and pepper. Place half of the flour in a bowl and add the yeast mixture. Mix to form a smooth but sticky dough. Add the remaining flour and mashed potato and knead vigorously. Place the dough in a bowl, cover and let rise in a warm place for 1 hour.
Divide the risen dough in half and spread it out with fingertips into 2 oiled baking sheets. Let the focaccias rise for 1 hour.
Preheat the oven to 425°F (220°C or Gas Mark 7). Sprinkle the rosemary over the focaccias and sprinkle with coarse salt. Bake for 20-25 minutes.
Remove from the oven and brush with the remaining olive oil. Serve immediately.

Yeast is a rising agent that works though fermentation, a process in which sugars are transformed into carbon dioxide in the case of breadmaking, or alcohol in the case of wine or spirits.

Preparation time **40 minutes**
Cooking time **50 minutes**
Level **easy**
Wine **Bardolino Chiaretto**

focaccia with cheese

Ingredients for 4 servings
Dough:
2⅓ cups plus 1 tbsp (10½ oz or 300 g) all-purpose flour
1⅔ cups (7 oz or 200 g) semolina flour
7 tbsps water
3 tbsps extra-virgin olive oil
1 lb (500 g) crescenza or other soft cheese
salt

Mix the two flours together with the water, olive oil and a pinch of salt until the dough is smooth. Cover with plastic wrap and let rest for 1 hour at room temperature. Preheat the oven to 485°F (250°C or Gas Mark 10). Roll out half of the dough into a very thin sheet and use it to line an oiled rimmed baking sheet.
Top with small spoonfuls of cheese. Roll out the remaining dough and use it to cover the cheese. Pinch the dough shut around the edges to seal. Poke small holes around the surface of the dough and drizzle with olive oil. Sprinkle with salt and bake for 5-7 minutes until browned on the top and bottom.

For a rich variation on Ligurian focaccia, try placing a few slices of very thinly sliced ham on top of the cheese filling.

Preparation time **15 minutes**
Cooking time **20 minutes**
Level **easy**
Wine **Pigato**

fried chickpea focaccias

Ingredients for 4 servings
Dough:

14 oz (400 g) canned chickpeas
1½ tsps active dry yeast
3/4 cup plus 1 tbsp (200 ml) water
3¼ cups (14 oz or 400 g) all-purpose flour
3 tbsps extra-virgin olive oil, salt
1 rosemary sprig, minced
6 cups (1½ l) peanut oil
coarse salt, butter

Puree the chickpeas in a food processor.
Prepare the dough following the recipe on page 384.
Add the chickpeas and half of the rosemary to the dough and mix well. Let rise for 20 minutes.
Roll out the dough into a thin sheet (about 1/5-inch 3 mm) and cut out 2½-inch (6 cm) rounds using a cookie cutter.
Heat the peanut oil in a large saucepan and, working in batches, fry the focaccias until golden.
Drain and dry on paper towels.
Sprinkle with salt and the remaining rosemary.
Serve very hot.

Serve these little focaccias with salami or cured meats and cheeses. Alternatively spread the focaccias with a fresh cheese and top with freshly ground pepper. For a thicker, softer variation, let the dough rise only after it has been rolled out and cut into rounds.

Preparation time **20 minutes**
Cooking time **10 minutes**
Level **easy**
Wine **Trentino Müller Thurgau**

puglian focaccia

Ingredients for 6 servings

Dough:

2 potatoes

salt

3¼ tsps (25 g) active dry yeast

4 cups (1 lb 1½ oz or 500 g) all-purpose flour

4 tbsps extra-virgin olive oil

Topping:

oregano

10 cherry tomatoes

1 tbsp pitted black olives

extra-virgin olive oil

coarse salt

Boil the potatoes in salted water, peel and mash with a potato ricer. Dissolve the yeast in a little warm water. Mound the flour on a work surface and make a well in the center. Add the potatoes, yeast mixture, a pinch of salt and enough water to form a smooth dough. Mix to combine, adjusting flour and water if necessary, and when the dough comes together knead vigorously until smooth. Form the dough into a ball and make an X-shaped incision on the top.
Cover and let rise for 2 hours, or until doubled in volume. Preheat the oven to 350°F (180°C or Gas Mark 4).
Oil a baking sheet and spread the dough onto the sheet until it is about 2½-inch (6 cm) thick.
Sprinkle over the oregano and place the cherry tomatoes and oliveson top at regular intervals, pressing them into the dough. Drizzle the focaccia with olive oil and sprinkle overa few pinches of coarse salt. Bake for 30 minutes, until the top of the focaccia is golden-brown.
Serve immediately.

Try substituting the tomatoes with grilled eggplant or porcini mushrooms, either fresh or preserved in oil.

Preparation time **40 minutes**
Cooking time **50 minutes**
Level **easy**
Wine **San Severo Bianco Spumante**

corn focaccia with pancetta

Ingredients for 6 servings
Dough:

3¼ tsps (25 g) active dry yeast
4 cups (1 lb 1½ oz or 500 g) all-purpose flour
4 tbsps (2 oz or 50 g) butter
salt and pepper
1/3 cup (2 oz or 50 g) finely ground cornmeal
5½ oz (150 g) pancetta, diced
3 tbsps extra-virgin olive oil
1 bunch mixed herbs, minced

Prepare the dough following the recipe on page 384. After the dough has risen, knead in 2 tablespoons of pancetta and all but 1 tablespoon of the cornmeal. Spread the dough onto an oiled baking sheet in a fairly thick layer.
Brush with olive oil and sprinkle over the remaining cornmeal. Fill a spray bottle with water and mist the focaccia from a distance of about 12 inches (30 cm).
Season with salt and let rise for 20 minutes in a warm place. Preheat the oven to 400°F (200°C or Gas Mark 6).
Bake the focaccia for 15 minutes, remove from the oven and top with the remaining pancetta and the minced herbs. Return to the oven and cook for another 10 minutes or until the pancetta begins to render and brown. Serve hot.

The term maize derives from the Arawak word mahiz. It was the term used by the pre-Colombian people who first offered corn to the conquistadors.

Preparation time **20 minutes**
Cooking time **25 minutes**
Level **easy**
Wine **Lambrusco di Sorbara**

schiaccia with onions and anchovies

Ingredients for 4 servings

Dough:

1¾ tsps (12 g) active dry yeast

3/4 cup plus 1 tbsp (200 ml) warm water

3¼ cups (14 oz or 400 g) all-purpose flour

4 tbsps extra-virgin olive oil

Topping:

3 tbsps extra-virgin olive oil

10 anchovies in salt, rinsed

3 red onions, thinly sliced, salt and pepper

1 bunch parsley, minced

Dissolve the yeast in a little warm water. Prepare the dough following the instructions on page 384.
Roll the dough into a ball and let rise for 1 hour.
Preheat the oven to 410°F (210°C or Gas Mark 6 ½).
Meanwhile, heat 2 tablespoons of olive oil in a frying pan and add the anchovies and onions. Season with pinches of salt and pepper and cook until the onions soften. Remove from the heat and set aside.
Spread the dough into an oiled, rimmed baking sheet. Top with the onion-anchovy mixture. Bake for 15 minutes, remove from the oven and sprinkle with the parsley.
Cut into squares and serve immediately.

⌐ To preserve anchovies at home, remove the head and guts from the fresh fish. Make a layer of coarse salt in a container and cover it with the fish fillets, cover the fish with coarse salt and continue making layers until all the fish have been used. Cover the final layer of fish with a thick layer of coarse salt.

Preparation time **30 minutes**
Cooking time **25 minutes**
Level **easy**
Wine **Vernaccia di San Gimignano**

potato-thyme focaccia

Ingredients for 4 servings

Dough:

1 small potato

salt

1¾ tsps (12 g) active dry yeast

3/4 cup plus 1 tbsp (200 ml) warm water

1 tsp sugar

2¾ cups (12½ oz or 350 g) all-purpose flour

4 tbsps extra-virgin olive oil, coarse salt

1 rosemary sprig, leaves only

2 thyme sprigs, leaves only

Boil the potato in salted water until tender. Drain, peel and mash with a ricer.
Dissolve the yeast in the warm water. Add a pinch of salt and the sugar. Mound the flour onto a work surface and make a well in the center. Pour the yeast mixture into the well. Add the mashed potato and begin to mix, using the fingertips. When the dough begins to come together, knead with the palms of the hands until smooth.
Cover the dough with a clean kitchen towel and let rise in a cool, dry place for 2-3 hours.
Roll out the dough on a lightly floured surface. Place the dough in an oiled rimmed baking sheet. Poke holes in the dough using the fingertips, brush with olive oil and sprinkle with coarse salt. Sprinkle over the rosemary and let rise for 1 hour in a warm place.
Preheat the oven to 400°F (200°C or Gas Mark 6).
Bake the focaccia for 20-25 minutes. Remove from the oven and serve immediately.

Potato focaccia my be served with soft cheeses or stuffed with prosciutto and fresh tomatoes.

Preparation time **15 minutes**
Cooking time **25 minutes**
Level **easy**
Wine **Prosecco di Conegliano Brut**

stuffed focaccia with ricotta, cherry tomatoes and basil

Ingredients for 6 servings

Dough:

3¼ tsps (25 g) active dry yeast

3½ cups (1 lb and 1½ oz or 500 g) bread flour

4 tbsps (2 oz or 50 g) butter

1 tsp salt

2 tbsps extra-virgin olive oil

Filling:

1 lb (500 g) ricotta

5 tbsps extra-virgin olive oil

salt and pepper

12 cherry tomatoes, halved

8 fresh basil leaves

Prepare the dough following the recipe on page 384. Preheat the oven to 350°F (180°C or Gas Mark 4). Beat together the ricotta and 2 tablespoons of olive oil. Season to taste with salt and pepper. Toss the tomatoes with pinches of salt and pepper and 2 tablespoons of olive oil. Roll the dough out into 2 rounds. Place one in an oiled round baking dish. Spread the ricotta mixture over the focaccia and top with the tomatoes.
Tear up the basil leaves and sprinkle them over the tomatoes. Cover with the remaining dough round, pinching the edges to seal.
Pierce the top with a fork and bake for 20 minutes. Remove from the oven and slice into wedges. Serve immediately.

The ricotta can be replaced with 9 oz (250 g) of sliced buffalo mozzarella and 2 tablespoons of capers.

Preparation time **30 minutes**
Cooking time **20 minutes**
Level **easy**
Wine **Prosecco di Conegliano e Valdobbiadene**

miniature buckwheat focaccias with fennel seeds

Ingredients for 6 servings

Dough:

1¾ tsps (12 g) active dry yeast

2⅓ cups plus 1 tbsp (10½ oz or 300 g) buckwheat flour

1⅔ cups (7 oz or 200 g) all-purpose flour

salt

2 tbsps fennel seeds

Dissolve the yeast in a little warm water.
Sift the 2 flours together on a clean work surface.
Add a pinch of salt and 1 tablespoon of fennel seeds and mix to combine. Make a well in the center and pour in the yeast mixture. Begin to mix with the fingertips, adding enough water to form a thick, even dough.
Knead vigorously until the dough becomes elastic.
Roll into a ball and let rise for 2 hours.
Preheat the oven to 400°F (200°C or Gas Mark 6).
Divide the risen dough into 6 small portions.
Smash down the dough using the palm of the hand to make rounds of medium thickness. Place the focaccias on a baking sheet lined with parchment paper and pierce with a fork. Sprinkle with the remaining fennel seeds.
Bake for 30 minutes, remove from the oven and cool slightly before serving.

Buckwheat is commonly used in northern European cooking as the grain grows better in cooler climates. Buckwheat bread has a characteristic acidity.

Preparation time **40 minutes**
Cooking time **30 minutes**
Level **easy**
Beer **Italian Pilsner**

focaccia with ciccioli

Ingredients for 6 servings

Dough:

3½ oz (100 g) scraps of pork back fat, diced

1/4 cup (2 oz or 50 g) lard

4 cups (1 lb 1½ oz or 500 g) all-purpose flour

1¼ tsps (10 g) active dry yeast

1 tbsp salt

Render the pork fat in 1 tablespoon of lard. Set aside and keep warm.
Mound the flour on a work surface and make a well at the center. Add the yeast, salt and enough warm water to form a smooth dough. Knead until the dough is elastic and then add the rendered pork fat and drippings.
Let rise for at least 30 minutes.
Preheat the oven to 400°F (200°C or Gas Mark 6). Grease a rimmed baking sheet with the remaining lard and spread the dough onto the baking sheet in a thick layer using the fingertips. Poke holes with the fingers around the surface of the dough.
Bake for 15 minutes, reduce the heat to 375°F (190°C or Gas Mark 5) and continue baking until golden-brown. Serve warm.

Ciccioli are made up of pork back scraps. The meat and fat are rendered for the lard and the remaining pieces, ciccioli, are smashed and dried. They are similar to Spanish and Latin American *chicharones*.

Preparation time **20 minutes**
Cooking time **30 minutes**
Level **medium**
Wine **Lambrusco Salamino di Santa Croce**

onion schiacciata

Ingredients for 4 servings

Topping:

5 white onions, thinly sliced

coarse salt

12½ oz (350 g) risen bread dough

1 tbsp lard

7 tbsps extra-virgin olive oil

Preheat the oven to 400°F (200°C or Gas Mark 6). Place the sliced onions in a colander and sprinkle over a few pinches of coarse salt. Let the onions sit until they begin to release moisture. Rinse and drain the onions. Place the dough on a floured work surface. Make an indentation in the center and add the lard and 3 tablespoons of olive oil. Knead the dough until the oil and lard have been incorporated. Spread the dough into an oiled rimmed baking sheet.
Top the dough with the onions and drizzle over the remaining olive oil. Bake for 10 minutes and reduce the heat to 350°F (180°C or Gas Mark 4) and bake for another 20 minutes. Remove the schiacciata from the oven when it is golden brown, and slice and serve immediately.

For a sweeter flavor use sweet red onions, such as Tropea, in place of the white onions. If desired, top the schiacciata with tuna in oil, drained and crumbled.

Preparation time **20 minutes**
Cooking time **30 minutes**
Level **easy**
Wine **Colli del Trasimeno Bianco**

focaccia with red onions and thyme

Ingredients for 6 servings

Dough:

2½ tsps active dry yeast

1¼ cups (300 ml) water

4 cups (1 lb 1½ oz or 500 g) all-purpose flour

salt

4½ tbsps extra-virgin olive oil

4 red onions, thinly sliced

2 thyme sprigs, leaves only

Dissolve the yeast in the water and mix it together with the flour, salt and 1½ tablespoons of olive oil. Knead the dough until smooth, place in an floured bowl and let rise for 20 minutes. Heat 2 tablespoons of olive oil in a large frying pan and add the onions. Season with a pinch of salt and cook over medium heat until soft. Let cool completely and then add the onions to the dough with half of the thyme leaves. Roll out the dough to a sheet ¾-inch (1½ cm) thick and use it to line an oiled baking sheet. Let rise for 30 minutes. Preheat the oven to 400°F (200°C or Gas Mark 6). Brush the focaccia with olive oil and sprinkle with the remaining thyme leaves and a pinch of salt. Bake for 20 minutes.

⌐ Top the onion focaccia with a few quartered cherry tomatoes for a light and fresh variation.

Preparation time **15 minutes**
Cooking time **20 minutes**
Level **easy**
Wine **Alto Adige Pinot Bianco**

miniature focaccias with goat's cheese and vegetables

Ingredients for 6 servings

Dough:

4 cups (1 lb 1½ oz or 500 g) all-purpose flour

1 tbsp lard

2 tbsps malt extract

2 tsps salt

1¼ cups (300 ml) water

2½ tsps active dry yeast

1½ tbsps extra-virgin olive oil

Filling:

14 oz (400 g) fresh goat's cheese, sliced

grilled mixed vegetables (zucchini, eggplants, tomatoes, onions)

oregano

extra-virgin olive oil

Smoked scamorza cheese or Emmenthal may be used in place of the goat's milk cheese. For a lactose-free variation, top the mini focaccias with slices of pancetta.

Mix together the flour, lard, malt extract, salt and half of the water in a large mixing bowl. Dissolve the yeast in the remaining water and add it to the mixture. Knead the dough vigorously until smooth and elastic, adding more water if the dough seems too firm. Cover with a kitchen towel and let rest for 20 minutes. Preheat the oven to 400°F (200°C or Gas Mark 6). Using a rolling pin, roll out the dough on a lightly floured surface. Cut out small rounds with a cookie cutter. Place the focaccias on an oiled baking sheet and let rise in a warm place for 30 minutes. Brush the focaccias with olive oil and bake for 10-12 minutes. Remove from the oven and let cool slightly. Top with a slice of goat's cheese, some grilled vegetables and sprinkle with oregano. Drizzle with olive oil and return to the oven for a few minutes, just enough to soften the cheese and heat the vegetables

Preparation time **20 minutes**
Cooking time **10 minutes**
Level **easy**
Wine **Prosecco di Conegliano Extra Dry**

urbino-style focaccia

Ingredients for 4 servings

Dough:

2⅓ cups plus 1 tbsp (10½ oz or 300 g) all-purpose flour

3 eggs

salt

1/2 cup (3½ oz or 100 g) lard

Mound the flour on a work surface and make a well in the center. Break the eggs into the well, add a pinch of salt and mix to form a smooth and dense dough. Cover with a clean kitchen towel and let rest for at least 30 minutes. Roll out the dough in a medium-thick layer and place chunks of lard over the dough.
Roll the dough up so that the lard remains on the inside and slice into small pieces, pinching the edges to make sure the lard stays inside. Let rest for about 1 hour in a cool place.
Roll out the pieces of dough into thin rounds and cook them in a non-stick frying pan until they begin to puff up and brown. Flip and cook the other side as well. Serve the focaccias immediately.

These flatbreads are excellent when filled with grilled vegetables or spreadable cheeses like stracchino.

Preparation time **25 minutes**
Cooking time **15 minutes**
Level **easy**
Wine **Bianchello del Metauro**

provençal focaccia

Ingredients for 6 servings

Dough:

3¼ tsps (25 g) active dry yeast

2 cups (9 oz or 250 g) all-purpose flour

3½ tbsps (2 oz or 50 g) butter

salt

extra-virgin olive oil

Topping:

6 tbsps extra-virgin olive oil

3 onions, sliced

2 garlic cloves, sliced

1 tbsp minced thyme

2 rosemary sprigs

10 anchovy fillets in oil, drained and halved lengthwise

1/2 cup (2 oz or 60 g) black olives

salt

Prepare the focaccia dough following the instructions on page. 382.
Heat half of the olive oil for the topping in a frying pan and sauté the onions. Cover the pan and cook over low heat for 30 minutes. Season with salt and add the garlic, thyme and 1 rosemary sprig. Continue cooking for another 5 minutes, then remove the rosemary and let the onions cool for 30 minutes.
Preheat the oven to 425°F (220°C or Gas Mark 7).
Roll out the dough and place it in an oiled baking tray. Spread the onions over the surface. Arrange the anchovies in diamond shapes over the onions.
Sprinkle over the olives and the leaves from the remaining rosemary sprig. Drizzle over the remaining oil.
Bake for 25 minutes, until golden.
Adjust salt and let cool before serving.

Preparation time **30 minutes**
Cooking time **1 hour 20 minutes**
Level **medium**
Wine **Riviera Ligure di Ponente Pigato**

artichoke focaccia

Ingredients for 6 servings

Dough:

3¼ tsps (25 g) active dry yeast

3½ cups (1 lb and 1½ oz or 500 g) bread flour

4 tbsps (2 oz or 50 g) butter

1 tsp salt

extra-virgin olive oil

Topping:

6 baby artichokes

juice of **1** lemon

4 tbsps extra-virgin olive oil

2 garlic cloves

1 bunch parsley, minced

coarse salt

For a hearty variation, add 7 oz (200 g) of pitted black olives to the focaccia before baking.

Prepare the dough following the recipe on page 384. Preheat the oven to 400°F (200°C or Gas Mark 6).
Trim the artichokes, removing the tough outer leaves and inner choke. Quarter them and soak in cold water acidulated with the lemon juice.
Heat 3 tablespoons of olive oil in a frying pan and brown the whole, unpeeled garlic cloves. Drain the artichokes and add them to the pan. Sauté for 10 minutes.
Roll out the dough and place in an oiled baking sheet. Top with the artichokes and sprinkle over the parsley and a few pinches of coarse salt.
Drizzle with olive oil and bake for 15 minutes.

Preparation time **20 minutes**
Cooking time **25 minutes**
Level **easy**
Wine **Friuli Aquileia Traminer**

cauliflower and cherry tomato focaccia

Ingredients for 6 servings

Dough:

3¼ tsps (25 g) active dry yeast

3½ cups (1 lb and 1½ oz or 500 g) bread flour

4 tbsps (2 oz or 50 g) butter

1 tsp salt

extra-virgin olive oil

Topping:

4 cups (14 oz or 400 g) cauliflower florets

salt and pepper

10 cherry tomatoes, quartered

3 tbsps extra-virgin olive oil

Prepare the dough following the recipe on page 384.
Preheat the oven to 400°F (200°C or Gas Mark 6).
Boil the cauliflower florets in salted water for 7-8 minutes. Drain and cool in a bowl of ice water, then drain and pat dry. Dress the tomatoes with pinches of salt and pepper and drizzle over 1 tablespoon of olive oil.
Roll out the dough and place it in an oiled, rimmed baking sheet. Top the focaccia with the cauliflower and tomatoes. Drizzle with olive oil and bake for 15 minutes.
Remove from the oven, slice and serve.

The cauliflower may be substituted with 2 thinly sliced sautéed onions

Preparation time **20 minutes**
Cooking time **25 minutes**
Level **easy**
Wine **Bolgheri Bianco**

stuffed herb focaccia with spinach and pancetta

Ingredients for 6 servings

Dough:

3¼ tsps (25 g) active dry yeast

3½ cups (1 lb and 1½ oz or 500 g) bread flour

4 tbsps (2 oz or 50 g) butter, 1 tsp salt

1 cup (1 oz or 20 g) minced thyme

1 cup (1 oz or 20 g) minced marjoram

extra-virgin olive oil

Filling:

1/2 lb (400 g) spinach, salt

2 tbsps extra-virgin olive oil

7 oz (200 g) pancetta, diced

1 cup (3½ oz or 100 g) grated Parmesan cheese

Prepare the dough following the recipe on page 384, adding in the minced herbs before the dough is kneaded. Preheat the oven to 350°F (180°C or Gas Mark 4). Blanch the spinach for 2 minutes in boiling salted water. Drain and transfer to a frying pan with the olive oil. Sauté briefly and remove from heat.
Render the pancetta for a few minutes in a frying pan, pour off the excess fat then add the pancetta to the spinach along with the Parmesan.
Roll out the dough into 2 rounds. Line the dough round into an oiled cake pan. Top with the spinach filling and cover with the remaining dough, pinching down around the edges to seal. Pierce the top of the focaccia with a fork and bake for 20 minutes. Slice and serve the focaccia hot.

For a vegetarian variation, substitute the pancetta with the same quantity of diced Emmenthal or Gruyère and mix it into the spinach filling.

Preparation time **30 minutes**
Cooking time **25 minutes**
Level **easy**
Wine **Alto Adige Schiava**

focaccia with mushrooms, catalogna chicory and taleggio

Ingredients for 6 servings

Dough:

3¼ tsps (25 g) active dry yeast

3½ cups (1 lb and 1½ oz or 500 g) bread flour

4 tbsps (2 oz or 50 g) butter

1 tsp salt, extra-virgin olive oil

Filling:

2 tbsps extra-virgin olive oil

1½ cups (5½ oz or 150 g) button mushrooms, thinly sliced

salt and pepper

3 stalks (3½ oz or 100 g) Catalogna chicory (see note), thinly sliced

7 oz (200 g) Taleggio, sliced

Catalogna is a kind of chicory with dark-green, serrated leaves and a bitter, peppery flavor. It could be replaced here by any other bitter green (broccoli rabe or turnip tops for example).

Prepare the dough following the recipe on page 384. Preheat the oven to 400°F (200°C or Gas Mark 6).
Heat the olive oil for the filling in a frying pan and sauté the mushrooms. Season to taste with salt and pepper. Blanch the chicory for a few minutes in boiling water, drain and squeeze out the excess water.
Roll out the dough and use it to line an oiled rimmed baking sheet. Top with the sautéed mushrooms, Taleggio and chicory. Bake for 15 minutes. Remove from the oven, slice and serve hot or warm, as desired.

Preparation time **20 minutes**
Cooking time **20 minutes**
Level **easy**
Wine **Rossese di Dolceacqua**

stuffed focaccia with artichokes and finocchiona

Ingredients for 6 servings

Dough:

1¾ tsps (12 g) active dry yeast, salt

3/4 cup plus 1 tbsp (200 ml) warm water

3¼ cups (14 oz or 400 g) all-purpose flour

3 tbsps extra-virgin olive oil

Topping:

7 oz (200 g) mozzarella, diced

2 ½ oz (70 g) pecorino, grated

5½ oz (150 g) artichokes in oil, drained and quartered

5 ½ oz (150 g) finocchiona salami, thinly sliced

1 tbsp fennel seeds

2 tbsps extra-virgin olive oil, salt

Finocchiona is a typical Tuscan salami. Its name and characteristic flavor come from the addition of wild fennel seeds. It could be replaced here with another salami.

Prepare the dough following the recipe on page 384.
Preheat the oven to 400°F (200°C or Gas Mark 6).
Place the diced mozzarella on a paper towel to dry.
Transfer to a mixing bowl and mix with the pecorino, artichokes and a pinch of salt.
Roll out three-quarters of the dough into a circle.
Line a 10-inch (26 cm) cake pan with the dough and top with the artichoke mixture. Cover the filling with a layer of finocchiona salami.
Roll out the remaining dough into a thin round and use it to cover the focaccia, pinching down around the edges to seal. Cover and let rise for 20 minutes.
Brush the top with 2 tablespoons of olive oil and sprinkle over the fennel seeds.
Bake for 25 minutes, remove from the oven and serve immediately.

Preparation time **15 minutes**
Cooking time **25 minutes**
Level **easy**
Beer **Irish Stout**

stuffed focaccia with broccoli and sausage

Ingredients for 6 servings

Dough:

3¼ tsps (25 g) active dry yeast

3½ cups (1 lb and 1½ oz or 500 g) bread flour

4 tbsps (2 oz or 50 g) butter

1 tsp salt, extra-virgin olive oil

Filling:

2 lbs (1 kg) broccoli florets, salt

9 oz (250 g) sausage

7 oz (200 g) caciocavallo, pecorino or provolone cheese, diced

red chili pepper flakes

3 tbsps extra-virgin olive oil

Prepare the dough following the recipe on page 384. Preheat the oven to 425°F (220°C or Gas Mark 7). Blanch the broccoli flowers in boiling salted water until tender, about 15 minutes. Drain and transfer to a bowl. Crumble in the sausage, add the caciocavallo and season with a pinch of salt and as much chili as desired. Roll out the dough into 2 rounds, ¼ inch (½ cm) in thickness. Line an oiled cake pan with one of the rounds and top the dough with the broccoli filling. Spread the filling into an even layer and cover with the remaining dough round. Pinch down the edges to seal and brush the top with the olive oil. Bake for 45 minutes or until golden-brown and cooked through.
Remove from the oven, slice and serve.

Preparation time **15 minutes**
Cooking time **1 hour**
Level **easy**
Wine **Torbato di Alghero Spumante**

stuffed focaccia with tomatoes and anchovies

Ingredients for 4 servings

Dough:

2½ tsps active dry yeast

1¼ cups (300 ml) water

4 cups (1 lb 1½ oz or 500 g) all-purpose flour

2 tbsps extra-virgin olive oil, salt

Filling:

5 tbsps extra-virgin olive oil

1 onion, diced, **3** anchovy fillets, salt

7 oz (200 g) cherry tomatoes, quartered

1 cup (3½ oz or 100 g) grated pecorino cheese

1 tbsp minced parsley

Prepare the dough following the instructions on page 384. Preheat the oven to 350°F (180°C or Gas Mark 4). Divide the dough into 2 parts and roll out 2 thin rounds. Heat 3 tablespoons of olive oil in a frying pan and add the onion, tomatoes and anchovies.
Sauté for 5 minutes over high heat. Season to taste with salt and add the parsley. Let cool.
Line one dough round into an oiled cake pan. Top with the tomato filling and sprinkle over the grated pecorino. Cover with the remaining dough round, pinching down the edges to seal. Brush the surface with the remaining olive oil and bake for 30 minutes.
Remove from the oven and serve immediately.

For a rich filling variation, top the tomato sauce with 4½ oz (125 g) diced fresh mozzarella and a few teaspoons of capers.

Preparation time **40 minutes**
Cooking time **35 minutes**
Level **easy**
Wine **Bianco di Scandiano**

savory tarts

Pizza

erbazzone

Ingredients for 6 servings

Dough:

3/4 cup plus 1 tbsp (3½ oz or 100 g) all-purpose flour

1/3 cup (2½ oz or 70 g) lard

warm milk

Filling:

2 lb (1 kg) Swiss chard

1 tab of butter, salt

2 oz (60 g) pancetta, diced

1 garlic clove, **1** onion, diced

1 bunch of parsley, minced

2 cups (7 oz or 200 g) grated Parmesan cheese

1/2 cup (2 oz or 60 g) breadcrumbs

4 eggs

2 oz (60 g) lardo (cured lard), thinly sliced

Preheat the oven to 300°F (150°C or Gas Mark 2).
Mix together the flour and the lard. Add a little warm milk to bind the dough, cover and let rest.
Boil the chard in salted water until tender. Drain, finely chop and squeeze out any excess water.
Meanwhile, melt a tab of butter in a pan and render the pancetta. Add the onion, whole garlic clove and parsley. Let the mixture brown briefly and add the chard.
Cook for 15 minutes.
Transfer the mixture to a bowl and mix in the grated Parmesan, breadcrumbs, eggs and a pinch of salt.
Roll out the dough into 2 thin sheets. Line a baking dish with half of the lardo, then line the pan with 1 sheet of dough. Spread the chard filling over the dough and top with the second sheet of dough. Cut away any excess dough. Pierce the top of the erbazzone with a fork and cover it with the remaining lardo. Bake for 30 minutes.

Preparation time **20 minutes**
Cooking time **45 minutes**
Level **easy**
Wine **Ortrugo**

zucchini tart with goat's cheese and pancetta

Ingredients for 4-6 servings

Dough:
1 2/3 cups (7 oz or 200 g) all-purpose flour
7 tbsps (3½ oz or 100 g) butter
salt

Filling:
2 garlic cloves
3 tbsps extra-virgin olive oil
2 medium zucchini, diced
4 eggs, salt and pepper
2 tbsps grated Parmesan cheese
3/4 cup plus 1 tbsp (200 ml) milk
7 tbsps heavy cream
3½ oz (100 g) fresh goat's milk cheese, diced
1/4 cup (1 oz or 30 g) pine nuts

Prepare the pastry following the instructions for pâte brisée on page 386. Cover with plastic wrap and refrigerate for at least 20 minutes. Preheat oven to 325°F (170°C). Sauté the garlic cloves in the olive oil until they begin to brown. Add the zucchini and season with salt. Cook until tender. Remove the garlic cloves and let cool. Beat the eggs and Parmesan together.
Add the milk and cream and season with salt and pepper. Puree the zucchini with the goat's cheese. Add the puree to the egg mixture.
Roll out the pâte brisée and place it in a tart tin. Pour in the zucchini filling and cut off any excess dough. Toast the pine nuts in a non-stick pan for a few minutes and sprinkle the over the tart.
Bake for 25-30 minutes and serve warm.

Preparation time **20 minutes**
Cooking time **40 minutes**
Level **medium**
Wine **Friuli Pinot Grigio**

eggplant and goat's cheese tart

Ingredients for 4 servings

Dough:

1²⁄₃ cups (7 oz or 200 g) all-purpose flour

1/2 cup plus 1 tbsp (3½ oz or 100 g) finely ground cornmeal

1/2 cup plus 1 tbsp (3½ oz or 100 g) quinoa flour

3/4 cup plus 1 tbsp (200 ml) water

4 tbsps corn oil, **1** tsp sugar, salt

1¾ tsps (12 g) active dry yeast

Filling:

2 small eggplants, sliced

salt and pepper

3 tbsps extra-virgin olive oil

1 onion, minced, **1** dried red chili pepper

1 bunch of cilantro, minced

9 oz (250 g) fresh goat's milk cheese

Mix together the ingredients for the dough and knead until smooth. Form into a ball, cover and let rise in a dry place for 3 hours.
Meanwhile, salt the eggplant slices and transfer to a colander. Place a plate on top, weigh down with some cans or other similar weights, and let sit for 30 minutes. Rinse the eggplant and dice it.
Preheat the oven to 425°F (220°C or Gas Mark 7).
Heat the olive oil in a frying pan, sauté the onions and crumble in the chile pepper. Add the eggplant and toss to coat. Cover and cook for 5 minutes.
Season with salt and pepper and add the minced cilantro.
Divide the dough in half and, using the fingertips, spread half into the bottom of an oiled cake pan. Crumble over the cheese and top with the eggplant mixture. Roll out the remaining dough and use it to cover the tart.
Pinch the edges to seal and bake for 25-30 minutes.
Remove from the oven and serve hot.

Preparation time **20 minutes**
Cooking time **50 minutes**
Level **medium**
Wine **Prosecco di Conegliano e Valdobbiadene Brut**

escarole and ricotta tart

Ingredients for 4 servings

Dough:

2 cups (9 oz or 250 g) whole-wheat flour
2 cups (9 oz or 250 g) all-purpose flour
3 tbsps extra-virgin olive oil
salt

Filling:

1 large head of escarole
2 tbsps extra-virgin olive oil
2 garlic cloves
1 handful of Gaeta or other black olives, pitted
1 handful of pine nuts
7 oz (200 g) ricotta, salt and pepper

Mix together the two flours, olive oil, salt and enough hot water to form a smooth dough. Let rest for 1 hour. Meanwhile, wash and thickly slice the escarole. Do not spin or dry the escarole.
Brown the whole garlic cloves in the olive oil and add the damp escarole. Cover and cook for 5 minutes. Add the olives and pine nuts and cook for another 10 minutes over low heat. Season to taste with salt and pepper.
Preheat the oven to 375°F (190°C or Gas Mark 5). Roll out the dough and line a baking dish with it. Pierce the dough with a fork. Beat the ricotta with a fork and spread it over the dough. Top with the escarole mixture and spread it into an even layer. Bake for about 25 minutes.
Let cool and remove from the pan before serving.

The term julienne refers to thinly slicing and ingredient into very thin, regular-sized strips.

Preparation time **25 minutes**
Cooking time **40 minutes**
Level **easy**
Wine **Greco di Tufo**

savory tart with peas, olives and pine nuts

Ingredients for 4 servings

Dough:

2⅓ cups plus 1 tbsp (10½ oz or 300 g) all-purpose flour

11 tbsps (5½ oz or 150 g) softened butter, diced

6 tbsps (90 ml) cold water, salt

Filling:

1 onion, minced

1 tbsp extra-virgin olive oil

3 cups (14 oz or 400 g) fresh peas

3/4 cup (180 ml) vegetable broth

1 egg, beaten, salt and pepper

10 pitted black olives

1 handful of pine nuts

Mound the flour on a work surface and make a well in the center. Place the butter and a pinch of salt in the well and work the dough with fingertips until it resembles coarse meal. Drizzle over the cold water and work the dough until it is smooth and white. Wrap in plastic wrap and refrigerate for 20 minutes. Preheat the oven to 350°F (180°C or Gas Mark 4). Sauté the onion in the olive oil until soft. Add the peas and cover with vegetable broth. Cook for 15 minutes, until tender. Puree the pea mixture and let cool. Season to taste with salt and pepper and stir in the egg and olives. Roll out the dough into a thin sheet and place it in a round tart pan. Spread the pea mixture over the dough and top with the pine nuts. Bake for 40 minutes.

Almonds may be used in place of the pine nuts in this recipe. Serve the tart with a fresh tomato salad if desired.

Preparation time **30 minutes**
Cooking time **55 minutes**
Level **easy**
Wine **Alto Adige Sylvaner**

puff pastry tart with feta

Ingredients for 8 servings

Dough:

1 lb and 1½ oz (500 g) puff pastry
7 tbsps (3½ oz or 100 g) butter, melted
1 lb and 1½ oz (500 g) feta cheese
9 oz (250 g) kefalotiri cheese (see note), grated
3/4 cup plus 2 tbsps (220 ml) milk
5 eggs, lightly beaten
1 bunch parsley, minced
pepper

Preheat the oven to 375°F (190°C or Gas Mark 5). To make the puff pastry at home, see recipe on page 385. Butter a rectangular baking dish and line it with three-quarters of the puff pastry.
Brush the pastry with a little melted butter. Prepare the filling: Mix together the two types of cheese, milk, eggs, parsley and pepper. Spread the filling over the puff pastry. Roll out the remaining puff pastry, brush it with the remaining butter and slice into thin strips. Decorate the top of the tart with the pastry strips and bake for 40 minutes. Remove from the oven, let cool and serve.

Kefalotiri is a Greek sheep's cheese made with raw milk. Sometimes it is made with a mix of goat and sheep's milk. It is an aged cheese that is easy to grate.

Preparation time **20 minutes**
Cooking time **40 minutes**
Level **easy**
Wine **Prosecco di Conegliano e Valdobbiadene Brut**

squash tart with pumpkin seeds

Ingredients for 6 servings
Dough:

3 zucchini, trimmed
1 white onion, finely chopped
2 tbsps extra-virgin olive oil
2 tbsps butter
2 carrots, peeled and diced
1/4 round, green-skinned winter squash or pumpkin, peeled, deseeded and diced
salt and pepper
2 cups (500 ml) hot vegetable broth
14 oz (400 g) pâte brisée (see page 386)
1 egg, thyme, chopped
1/4 cup (1¾ oz or 50 g) pumpkin seeds

Preheat oven to 375°F (190°C).
Slice the zucchini lengthwise into quarters and cut out the seedy white center. Dice the green part and set aside. Sauté the onion in a frying pan with the oil and butter, add the carrots and then the pumpkin. Season with pinches of salt and pepper. Pour over the hot broth, cover and cook for 7 minutes. Add the zucchini and cook until tender. Remove from the heat and let cool.
Roll the pâte brisée out on a floured work surface to a 1/5-inch (4 mm) thickness. Line a floured tart tin with the dough and pierce the base with a fork.
Mix the egg and thyme with the vegetable filling and pour into the pastry. Sprinkle with pumpkin seeds and bake for about 40 minutes. Remove from the oven, let cool slightly and serve warm.

For a more substantial filling, add 3 diced potatoes to the sauté of pumpkin, zucchini and carrots.

Preparation time **25 minutes**
Cooking time **50 minutes**
Level **easy**
Wine **Gambellara**

spinach and grana tart

Ingredients for 4 servings

Dough:

4 tbsps (2 oz or 50 g) butter
1 onion, minced
2¾ lbs (1⅓ kg) spinach, chopped
salt
2 eggs
2/3 cup (150 ml) heavy cream
10½ oz (300 g) pâte brisée dough (see recipe page 386)
6 tbsps grated Trentingrana or Parmesan cheese

Preheat the oven to 400°F (200°C or Gas Mark 6).
Melt the butter in a large frying pan and add the onion. When the onion begins to brown, add the spinach and stir to coat the leaves with butter. Season with a pinch of salt, cover and cook for a few minutes.
Meanwhile, beat the eggs in a bowl and add the cream. Divide the dough in half and roll it out into thin rounds, about 9-inch in diameter.
Line a tart pan with one of the rounds and fill it with the sautéed spinach. Sprinkle over the cheese and pour over the egg mixture. Top with the remaining dough round and fold over the edges to seal.
Bake for 30 minutes, remove from the oven and serve warm.

For a richer filling, add a few tablespoons of ricotta to the egg and cream mixture. For a more delicate tart, omit the onions and simply steam the spinach.

Preparation time **15 minutes**
Cooking time **40 minutes**
Level **easy**
Wine **Trentino Müller Thurgau**

savory spinach bread with feta

Ingredients for 4 servings

Dough:

3 eggs

salt and pepper

7 tbsps (100 ml) milk

1⅓ cups plus 2 tbsps (6½ oz or 180 g) all-purpose flour

1 tsp baking powder

6 tbsps extra-virgin olive oil

7 oz (200 g) feta cheese, diced

1 handful of spinach, chopped

2 tbsps grated Gruyère cheese

Preheat the oven to 350°F (180°C or Gas Mark 4). Beat the eggs with pinches of salt and pepper in a mixing bowl and whisk in the milk. Sift in the flour and baking powder and stir to obtain a smooth batter. Add the olive oil and the feta to the batter. Mix in the spinach and Gruyère. Butter and flour a loaf pan and pour in the batter. Bake for 50 minutes. Let cool, unmold and serve.

The spinach may be replaced with any leafy green vegetable in season, and the Gruyère with any other cheese that melts easily.

Preparation time **30 minutes**
Cooking time **50 minutes**
Level **easy**
Wine **Trentino Müller Thurgau**

chicken, sweet corn and lentil pie

Ingredients for 6 servings

Dough:

2¾ cups plus 1 tbsp (350 g) all-purpose flour

6 tbsps (3 oz or 80 g) margarine, **1** egg

1 cup (250 ml) water

Filling:

2 skinless chicken breasts

1 tbsp extra-virgin olive oil, salt

1 onion, julienned

1/3 cup plus 1 tbsp (3½ oz or 100 g) ready-made tomato sauce

2/3 cup (5½ oz or 150 g) canned sweet corn, drained

2 tomatoes, diced

1/2 cup (3½ oz or 100 g) cooked lentils

1 jar of hearts of palm, drained and sliced

1 tsp cornstarch

Mix together all of the ingredients for the dough to form a smooth, dry dough. Wrap in plastic wrap and refrigerate for at least 20 minutes. Poach the chicken breasts in a saucepan of boiling salted water until cooked through. Drain, reserving 2 cups (500 ml) of the cooking liquid, and let the chicken cool. Slice the chicken into thin strips. Sauté the onion in the olive oil and add in the tomato sauce. Add the sweet corn, tomatoes, lentils and hearts of palm. Pour over the reserved cooking liquid and add the chicken. Season with salt and let the liquid cook off. When most of the liquid has evaporated, add the cornstarch dissolved in a little cold water and remove from the heat. Preheat the oven to 350°F (180°C or Gas Mark 4). Roll out the dough into a very large thin sheet. Place it on an oiled baking sheet so that half of the dough hangs off the sheet. Place the filling on the dough and fold the excess over the top of the filling. Seal the edges and cut small holes in the top of the dough to let the steam escape during baking. Bake for 25 minutes, until the surface is golden-brown. Cut the pie into squares and serve hot.

Preparation time **20 minutes**
Cooking time **1 hour 10 minutes**
Level **medium**
Wine **Bardolino Chiaretto**

savory pumpkin and chickpea strudel

Ingredients for 6 servings

Dough:
1¼ cups (5½ oz or 150 g) all-purpose flour
3 tbsps (1½ oz or 40 g) butter, melted
salt

Filling:
2 tbsps extra-virgin olive oil
1/2 white onion, diced
14 oz (400 g) pumpkin, peeled, deseeded and diced
1¼ cups (300 ml) hot vegetable broth
1 cup (5½ oz or 150 g) cooked chickpeas
1 thyme sprig, leaves only
salt and pepper, butter

Place the flour into a bowl and pour over the melted butter. Add a little water and a pinch of salt. Mix, adding more water if necessary, until a smooth dough forms. Roll the dough into a ball, cover with plastic wrap and refrigerate. Heat the olive oil in a frying pan and sauté the onion. Add the pumpkin and cook over low heat for 10 minutes, adding a little hot broth from time to time. Add the chickpeas and thyme and season to taste with salt and pepper. Cook for another 5 minutes until the pumpkin is quite soft.
Preheat the oven to 375°F (190°C or Gas Mark 5). Roll out the dough on a lightly floured work surface. Spread the pumpkin mixture over the dough and roll it up like a jelly roll. Transfer the strudel to a buttered baking sheet and brush the top of the strudel with melted butter. Make small diagonal incisions along the top of the strudel. Bake for 30 minutes, remove from the oven and let cool completely. Serve the strudel sliced along the diagonal.

⌐Pumpkin flesh can be used to calm skin irritations and the rind is said to help heal minor burns.

Preparation time **20 minutes**
Cooking time **1 hour 30 minutes**
Level **easy**
Wine **Riviera Ligure di Ponente Pigato**

savory san vito tart

Ingredients for 4-6 servings

Dough:

4 cups (1 lb 1½ oz or 500g) all-purpose flour

3¼ tsps (25 g) active dry yeast, salt

2 tbsps extra-virgin olive oil

Filling:

3 tbsps extra-virgin olive oil

1 onion, finely diced

1 bunch of basil, minced

1 bunch of parsley, minced

1 rosemary sprig, salt and pepper

10½ oz (300 g) ground beef

3 tbsps white wine

1 egg yolk, beaten

3 ripe tomatoes, peeled and pureed

3½ oz (100 g) caciocavallo, diced

1 tbsp grated pecorino cheese

Mix together 3/4 cup (3½ oz or 100 g) of the flour with the yeast dissolved in a little warm water. Form the dough into a ball and let rest for 2 hours. Add the remaining flour, a pinch of salt and the olive oil and knead to form a smooth dough. Let rest for 1 hour.
Preheat the oven to 400°F (200°C or Gas Mark 6).
Sauté the onion in the olive oil with the basil and parsley. Add the rosemary sprig and the beef and brown. Season to taste with salt and add the wine. Add the tomatoes and cook over low heat for 30 minutes, adding a little water if the mixture begins to dry out. Remove the rosemary sprig and stir in the caciocavallo and pecorino.
Roll out the dough into 2 rounds, one slightly larger than the other. Place the larger of the two in an oiled pie pan. Pour over the filling and smooth with a spatula.
Cover the tart with the remaining sheet of dough, and brush the surface with the beaten egg yolk.
Bake for 20 minutes, let cool slightly and serve.

Preparation time **40 minutes**
Cooking time **60 minutes**
Level **easy**
Wine **Bianco d'Alcamo**

olive bread with gruyère

Ingredients for 4 servings

Dough:

3 eggs

7 tbsps (100 ml) milk

1⅓ cup plus 2 tbsps (6½ oz or 180 g) all-purpose flour

1 tsp baking powder, salt and pepper

6 tbsps extra-virgin olive oil

2 oz (50 g) goat's milk cheese, chopped

4 tbsps grated Gruyère cheese

10 black and green olives

2 tbsps (1 oz or 20 g) butter

Preheat the oven to 350°F (180°C or Gas Mark 4).
Beat the eggs and the milk in a bowl with salt and pepper.
Sift in the flour and baking powder and add the olive oil and goat's cheese. Add the Gruyère and stir gently.
Rinse and dry the olives and dust them lightly with flour. Add to the batter.
Butter and flour a loaf pan and pour in the batter.
Bake for 45 minutes.
Remove from the oven, let cool and unmold.
Serve warm.

Try making this bread with asparagus instead of olives. Blanch 10 asparagus stalks in salted water for 3 minutes. Cool and dust with flour. Pour a third of the batter into a prepared loaf pan and top with 5 asparagus stalks. Cover with another third of the batter and top with the remaining asparagus. Pour over the rest of the batter and bake for 45 minutes.

Preparation time **15 minutes**
Cooking time **45 minutes**
Level **easy**
Wine **Roero Arneis**

spinach crescioni

Ingredients for 4-6 servings

Dough:
3¼ cups (500 g) all-purpose flour
5 tbsps lard
salt, milk

Filling:
1 garlic clove
7 oz (200 g) lardo (cured lard)
1 pinch of pepper
9 oz (250 g) spinach, salt

Crescioni differ slightly from piadinas because the edges are closed, while a piadina is simply folded over. Traditionally crescioni were filled with wild greens. Variations on this recipe are endless: Crescioni can be filled with squash, potatoes, tomatoes, cabbage or cheese.

Mound the flour on a wooden board and make a well in the center. Add the lard and a pinch of salt to the center of the well and mix. Gradually add enough milk to form a smooth and uniform dough. Work the dough quickly, otherwise air pockets may form during cooking.
Cover the dough with a clean kitchen towel and let rest for about an hour. Meanwhile mince the garlic and lardo together with the pepper. Bring a large pot of salted water to a boil. Add spinach and boil for 2 to 3 minutes. Drain, squeeze out excess water and chop.
In a large frying pan render the lardo and garlic mixture and then add the spinach. Salt to taste. On a floured surface roll out the dough into circles 8 inches (22 cm) in diameter. Place a few spoonfuls of filling on each circle and fold in half. Using a fork press the dough closed. Cook the crescioni on a griddle or in non-stick frying pan until both sides are golden-brown.

Preparation time **20 minutes**
Cooking time **30 minutes**
Level **easy**
Wine **Colli Piacentini Gutturnio**

potato and asiago quiche

Ingredients for 6 servings

Dough:

9 oz (250 g) pâte brisée dough (see page 386)
3 potatoes, salt and pepper
3 eggs
7 tbsps heavy cream
2 tbsps grated Parmesan cheese
nutmeg
1 bunch of spinach
10½ oz (300 g) Asiago cheese, diced
5 slices of ham
poppy seeds

Preheat the oven to 375°F (190°C or Gas Mark 5).
Roll out the dough and place it in an oiled tart tin.
Pierce the dough with a fork.
Boil the potatoes in salted water until tender. Peel and slice into rounds.
Beat the eggs with the cream and Parmesan. Season with a grating of fresh nutmeg and pinches of salt and pepper.
Make alternating layers of the potato slices, spinach, Asiago and ham. Add a little egg mixture to each layer until the egg is used up. Finish with a layer of ham and sprinkle with poppy seeds.
Bake for 45 minutes and let cool before serving.

Asiago is a cow's milk cheese from the Veneto region, and can be found fresh and aged. It can be replaced in this recipe by Parmesan or an aged pecorino.

Preparation time **30 minutes**
Cooking time **45 minutes**
Level **easy**
Wine **Trentino Müller Thurgau**

phyllo tart with zucchini and escarole

Ingredients for 6 servings

Dough:

2-3 garlic cloves, peeled
2 tbsps extra-virgin olive oil
1 head of escarole, roughly chopped
salt and pepper
5 sheets of phyllo dough (about 9 oz or 250 g)
2 zucchini, thinly sliced

Brown the whole garlic cloves in the olive oil. Remove the garlic from the pan and add the escarole. Cover and cook for 10 minutes over low heat. Season to taste with salt and pepper.
Oil a baking dish and line it with 3 sheets of phyllo dough. Top with the escarole, drained of any excess water, and layer over the zucchini. Drizzle with olive oil and season with pinches of salt and pepper.
Cover with the remaining sheets of phyllo dough and bake for 12-15 minutes. Serve immediately.

Phyllo dough is a type of very thin puff pastry which cooks quickly. It may be fried or baked. It is often used for preparing typical Middle Eastern sweets, like pastry parcels that are filled with pistachios and walnuts and dipped in sugar syrup. It is an ideal base for sweet and savory snacks or tarts.

Preparation time **10 minutes**
Cooking time **25 minutes**
Level **easy**
Wine **Vermentino di Gallura**

savory ricotta and salami pie

Ingredients for 6 servings

Dough:

1 2/3 cups (7 oz or 200 g) all-purpose flour

2 eggs

1 tbsp sugar

1 tbsp extra-virgin olive oil, salt

Filling:

14 oz (400 g) aged goat's milk cheese, grated

10 1/2 oz (300 g) ricotta

5 1/2 oz (150 g) salami, diced

6 eggs

parsley, minced

Mound the flour on a work surface and make a well at the center. Break the eggs into the well and add the sugar, olive oil and salt. Stir with fingertips until the dough comes together and then knead vigorously until smooth. Cover with a kitchen towel and let rest.
Meanwhile, mix together the goat's cheese, ricotta, salami, eggs and parsley. Stir to combine.
Roll out the dough into 2 rounds. Place one sheet of dough into a cake pan lined with parchment paper.
Pour in the filling and level it off with a spatula.
Cut the remaining dough into strips and form a lattice over the top. Pinch the edges and seal. Bake for 1 hour and cool to room temperature before serving.

Preparation time **30 minutes**
Cooking time **1 hour**
Level **medium**
Wine **Lambrusco di Sorbara**

potato and porcini quiche

Ingredients for 6 servings
Dough:

2 medium potatoes, peeled and diced

salt and pepper

5½ oz (150 g) pancetta, diced

2 tbsps extra-virgin olive oil

7 oz (200 g) fresh or frozen porcini mushrooms, diced

1 garlic clove

2 eggs

1 cup (250 ml) milk

3 oz (80 g) Emmenthal cheese, grated

9 oz (250 g) puff pastry

Preheat the oven to 400°F (200°C or Gas Mark 6).
Boil the potatoes in salted water until tender. Drain and set aside. Brown the pancetta in a frying pan with a little olive oil. Pour off most of the fat and add the pancetta to the potatoes.
Sauté the mushrooms and the garlic clove in the frying pan, adding a little more olive oil if necessary. Cook until just tender. Season to taste with salt.
Whisk together the eggs, milk, Emmenthal and pinches of salt and pepper in a mixing bowl.
Line a 10-inch (26 cm) diameter tart pan with parchment paper and top with the puff pastry.
Place the potato mixture and the mushrooms in the tart shell and pour over the milk and egg mixture.
Bake for 30 minutes. Let cool slightly before serving.

Preparation time **30 minutes**
Cooking time **40 minutes**
Level **easy**
Wine **Alto Adige Pinot Nero**

savory tarts

savory cheesecake

Ingredients for 4 servings

Dough:

5 medium potatoes
salt
1 shallot, minced
4 tbsps extra-virgin olive oil
3 eggs, beaten
5½ oz (150 g) stracchino or other soft, fresh, spreadable cheese, chopped
3 tbsps breadcrumbs

Preheat the oven to 350°F (180°C or Gas Mark 4).
Boil the potatoes in salted water until tender, drain, peel and mash. Season to taste with salt.
Sauté the shallot in the olive oil and stir in the mashed potatoes. Remove from heat and let cool slightly.
Add the eggs and the stracchino cut into small pieces. Mix to form a smooth batter.
Pour the batter into a cake pan and sprinkle with breadcrumbs. Bake for 30 minutes.

Do not keep potatoes for more than one day after they have been cooked. They contain solanium, a toxic substance that is broken down during cooking but reforms after 12 hours.
This savory cake makes an ideal dish for a picnic or an informal, outdoor lunch.

Preparation time **20 minutes**
Cooking time **50 minutes**
Level **easy**
Wine **Bardolino Chiaretto**

savory tart with ricotta, herbs and fresh tomatoes

Ingredients for 6 servings

Dough:

2⅓ cup plus 1 tbsp (10½ oz or 300 g) all-purpose flour

8 tbsps (4 oz or 120 g) butter, diced

1 egg

salt

Filling:

14 oz (400 g) ricotta

2 eggs

2 tbsps minced fresh herbs (basil, marjoram, thyme, parsley)

3 tbsps grated Parmesan cheese

salt and pepper

4 ripe tomatoes, thinly sliced

extra-virgin olive oil

oregano

Quickly mix together the flour, butter, egg and salt, adding a little cold water if the dough seems too dry.
Form into a ball, cover with plastic wrap and refrigerate for 30 minutes.
Preheat the oven to 350°F (180°C or Gas Mark 4).
In a mixing bowl, stir together the ricotta, eggs, herbs and Parmesan. Season with pinches of salt and pepper.
Line a 10-inch (26 cm) diameter tart pan with parchment paper. Roll out the dough into a thin sheet and use it to line the prepared pan, making a high border around the edges. Fill the crust with the ricotta mixture and top with a layer of tomato slices. Drizzle with olive oil and sprinkle with pinches of salt and oregano.
Bake for 25-30 minutes.

Preparation time **25 minutes**
Cooking time **30 minutes**
Level **easy**
Wine **Roero Arneis**

pumpkin flatbread with leek and tofu

Ingredients for 6 servings

Dough:

1/2 pumpkin or other winter squash, peeled, deseeded and sliced

2 tsps (15 g) active dry yeast

1/2 cup (120 ml) lukewarm water

2 tbsps sunflower oil

2 cups (9 oz or 250 g) all-purpose flour

Filling:

1 leek, chopped

1 tbsp extra-virgin olive oil

1 cup (7 oz or 200 g) crumbled tofu

Preheat oven to 350°F (180°C). Roast the pumpkin slices in the oven for 20 minutes. Weigh 9 oz (250 g) of the roasted squash and puree it in a food processor.
Dissolve the yeast in lukewarm water and add the sunflower oil. Mix the flour with the yeast mixture then add the pureed squash. Knead to form a smooth dough. Let rest for 1 hour.
Knead the dough again and roll into a 1/2-inch (1 cm) thick sheet. Line a round baking dish with the dough and let rise for another 30 minutes. Preheat the oven to 325°F (170°C or Gas Mark 3). Bake for 40 minutes.
Meanwhile, sauté the leek in a frying pan with the olive oil. As soon as it becomes translucent, add the tofu and cook over low heat for 10 minutes.
Remove the pumpkin flatbread from the oven and let cool slightly on a wire rack. Slice in half horizontally. Spread one layer with the leek and tofu mixture, then top with the other layer. Return to the oven for 5 more minutes. Serve warm.

Leeks are a very healthy food. They contain vitamins B and C, iron, calcium, phosphorus, magnesium, potassium and manganese. Like garlic and onions, leeks strengthen the immune system and are rich in antioxidants.

Preparation time **30 minutes**
Cooking time **1 hour 15 minutes**
Level **easy**
Wine **Ribolla Gialla**

vegetable tart with raisins and pine nuts

Ingredients for 4 servings
Dough:

2⅓ cups plus 1 tbsp (10½ oz or 300 g) all-purpose flour

9 tbsps (4½ oz or 125 g) butter, softened

2 eggs, separated, salt

Filling:

3 small artichokes

juice of **1** lemon, **1** lb (500 g) peas

1 lb (500 g) spinach

3 medium celery stalks, chopped

5½ oz (150 g) baby fennel or fennel bulb, chopped

1 onion, minced, salt and pepper

3 tbsps extra-virgin olive oil, **1** mint leaf

1 basil leaf

1/4 cup (1 oz or 30 g) raisins

1/4 cup (1 oz or 30 g) pine nuts

Mound the flour on a work surface and make a well in the center. Add the egg yolks into the well and add the salt and butter. Stir to form a dough and then knead vigorously until smooth. Cover with a kitchen towel and let rest for 1 hour. Preheat the oven to 350°F (180°C or Gas Mark 4). Meanwhile, remove the tough outer leaves and the choke from the artichokes and soak in cold water acidulated with a little lemon juice. Drain and thinly slice. Blanch the artichokes, peas, spinach, celery and fennel in lightly salted water, then drain. Heat the olive oil in a frying pan and add the onion. Sauté briefly and add the blanched vegetables, mint and basil. Soak the raisins for 5 minutes in a little warm water. Drain and squeeze out the excess liquid. Mix together the raisins and pine nuts, season to taste with salt and pepper and add to the vegetables. Roll out the dough into 2 rounds. Line an oiled baking dish with one dough round, top with the vegetable mixture and cover with the remaining dough. Brush the dough with a little lightly beaten egg white and bake for 25 minutes. Serve the tart hot or warm.

Preparation time **20 minutes**
Cooking time **45 minutes**
Level **easy**
Wine **Corvo di Casteldaccia Rosato**

zucchini and pecorino tart tatin

Ingredients for 4 servings

Dough:

1 garlic clove, smashed
1 tbsp extra-virgin olive oil
3 zucchini, julienned
salt and pepper
4 tbsps corn oil
2 tbsps slivered almonds
5½ oz (150 g) mild, soft pecorino cheese, shaved
9 oz (250 g) puff pastry

Preheat the oven to 375°F (190°C or Gas Mark 5). Brown the garlic in the olive oil. Remove the garlic and add the zucchini.
Sauté for 5 minutes over high heat and season to taste with salt and pepper. Brush 4 small tart tins with the corn oil. Spread a thin layer of almonds over the bottom. Top with the zucchini and shaved pecorino.
Roll out the puff pastry and cut out rounds the same size as the tart tins. Top the tarts with the pastry and press down around the edge to seal.
Bake for 15 minutes, remove from heat and invert the tarts onto plates before serving.

While the traditional tart tatin filling is apples, they can be sweet or savory. The filling in these tarts is placed on the bottom of the pan while the crust on the top, and then the tarts are inverted before serving.

Preparation time **20 minutes**
Cooking time **35 minutes**
Level **easy**
Wine **Roero Arneis**

savory ham, olive and gruyère pie

Ingredients for 6 servings

Dough:

2 oz (50 g) ricotta

4 tbsps (2 oz or 50 g) butter, softened

4 egg yolks

1/2 cup (120 ml) white wine

1¼ cups (5½ oz or 150 g) all-purpose flour

1/2 tsp baking powder

5 tbsps grated Parmesan cheese

3½ oz (100 g) Gruyère cheese, shaved

30 pitted green olives, halved

7 oz (200 g) ham, diced

salt and pepper

Preheat the oven to 400°F (200°C or Gas Mark 6). Beat together the ricotta and butter to obtain a smooth cream. Add the egg yolks and wine, and sift in the flour and baking powder. Mix in the Parmesan, Gruyère, olives and ham. Season to taste with salt and pepper. Butter and flour a cake pan and pour in the batter. Smooth the surface with a spatula and bake for 45 minutes. Remove from the oven and let cool just slightly. Slice the pie and serve hot.

⌐ The ricotta may be replaced by fresh robiola or any other soft, mild cheese.

Preparation time **15 minutes**
Cooking time **45 minutes**
Level **easy**
Wine **Pomino Bianco**

zucchini, potato and ricotta tart

Ingredients for 4-6 servings

Dough:
- 4 cups (1 lb 1½ oz or 500 g) flour
- 3 tbsps extra-virgin olive oil
- 2/3 cup (150 ml) water
- zest of 1 lemon
- 1 tsp salt

Filling:
- 14 oz (400 g) ricotta
- 5 tbsps minced mint leaves
- 2 medium potatoes, peeled and thinly sliced
- salt and pepper
- 1 lb (500 g) zucchini, sliced
- 6 tbsps extra-virgin olive oil
- sesame seeds

Preheat the oven to 350°F (180°C or Gas Mark 4). Mix together the ingredients for the dough and form into a ball. Roll out the dough into 2 thin sheets. Oil a baking sheet and top with 1 sheet of dough. Mix together the ricotta and mint. Spread the potatoes over the dough in a thin layer. Season with salt and pepper and top with spoonfuls of the ricotta mixture. Layer the zucchini slices over the ricotta and season again with salt and pepper. Top with spoonfuls of ricotta and mint and cover with the remaining sheet of dough. Brush the dough with olive oil and top with sesame seeds. Bake for 30 minutes, remove from the oven and cut into squares before serving.

Preparation time **20 minutes**
Cooking time **30 minutes**
Level **easy**
Wine **Dolcetto di Dogliani**

robiola, salmon and dill tart

Ingredients for 6 servings

Dough:

2⅓ cups plus 1 tbsp (10½ oz or 300 g) all-purpose flour

7 tbsps dry white wine

5 tbsps extra-virgin olive oil

2 tsps salt

Filling:

10½ oz (300 g) robiola or other soft mild cheese

3½ tbsps heavy cream

1 bunch of fresh dill, minced

6½ oz (180 g) smoked salmon, thinly sliced

salt and pepper

Preheat the oven to 350°F (180°C or Gas Mark 4).
Mix together all of the ingredients for the pastry to form a smooth dough. Roll into a ball and cover with plastic wrap. Refrigerate for 20 minutes.
Line a 10-inch (26 cm) diameter tart pan with parchment paper. Roll out the dough into a thin sheet and use it to line the prepared pan. Pierce the crust with a fork and bake for 10-12 minutes, until the crust just begins to color. Remove from the oven and let cool.
Mix together the robiola, cream and half of the dill. Julienne half of the smoked salmon slices and add them to the robiola mixture. Season to taste with salt and pepper and pour the filling into the cooled tart crust. Roll the remaining salmon slices into curls and use them to garnish the tart. Sprinkle with minced dill and serve.

Preparation time **30 minutes**
Cooking time **10 minutes**
Level **easy**
Wine **Friuli Collio Sauvignon**

couscous tart with feta

Ingredients for 6 servings

Dough:

3/4 cup plus 1 tbsp (3½ oz or 100 g) whole-wheat flour
1 cup (4 oz or 120 g) all-purpose flour
1/2 tsp baking powder, salt
3 tbsps peanut oil

Filling:

3 tbsps extra-virgin olive oil
1 shallot, minced
1/2 cup plus 1 tbsp (3½ oz or 100 g) couscous
1¼ cups (300 ml) hot vegetable broth
1/2 onion, diced, **2** carrots, diced
1 celery stalk, diced
2 small zucchini, diced, salt and pepper
5½ oz (150 g) feta, crumbled
1 bunch of parsley, minced

Sift the two flours and baking powder into a mixing bowl. Add the salt, peanut oil and enough water to form a smooth dough. Knead the dough until elastic, wrap in plastic wrap and let rest in the refrigerator. Preheat the oven to 400°F (200°C or Gas Mark 6). Heat 1 tablespoon olive oil in a saucepan and add the shallot. Let soften and then add the couscous. Let the couscous toast for 1 minute, then add the vegetable broth. Cover and cook for 2 minutes. Remove from heat and cool, covered. Break up the couscous with a fork and crumble it into an oiled baking dish. Heat the remaining olive oil in a frying pan and brown the onion. Add the carrots, and sauté briefly. Add the celery and zucchini. Season to taste with salt and pepper and cook for 5 minutes, adding a little water if necessary. Add the vegetable sauté to the couscous and stir to combine. Roll out the dough into a thin sheet. Line a round baking dish or pie pan with the dough and pierce it with a fork. Fill with the couscous mixture and bake for 30 minutes. Let cool and top with the feta and parsley.

Preparation time **30 minutes**
Cooking time **35 minutes**
Level **easy**
Wine **Fiano di Avellino**

swiss chard tart

Ingredients for 4 servings

Dough:

2 cups (9 oz or 250 g) all-purpose flour

9 tbsps (4½ oz or 125 g) butter

3 tbsps water

Filling:

2 tbsps extra-virgin olive oil

1 fennel bulb, thinly sliced

1 leek, thinly sliced, salt and pepper

6 oz (175 g) Swiss chard

2½ oz (70 g) soft, fresh, spreadable cheese

3 eggs

3/4 cup plus 1 tbsp (200 ml) heavy cream

Preheat the oven to 400°F (200°C or Gas Mark 6).
Pulse the flour and butter in a food processor and add enough water to form a smooth and elastic dough.
Roll into a ball and wrap in plastic wrap.
Refrigerate for 20 minutes.
Roll out the dough into a thin sheet and use it to line a round baking dish. Cover with parchment paper and fill with pie weights or a layer of uncooked rice or beans. Bake for 15 minutes. Remove the rice and the parchment paper and bake for another 10 minutes.
Meanwhile, heat the olive oil in a large frying pan, add the fennel and leek and season with salt and pepper. Cover and cook for 20 minutes. Steam the chard until tender. Spread the cooked vegetables over the tart crust and drop over spoonfuls of cheese. Beat together the eggs and cream and season with salt and pepper. Pour the mixture over the vegetables and bake for 40 minutes. Serve the tart hot or warm.

⌐ The Italian word for fennel is finocchio. This is the origin of the Italian verb infinocchiare, meaning to cheat. In the past, wine vendors would offer a slice of raw fennel to buyers while tasting wine because it can cover up or falsify flavors, making an undrinkable wine seem acceptable.

Preparation time **15 minutes**
Cooking time **1 hour 5 minutes**
Level **easy**
Wine **Malvasia Istriana**

savory potato and bacon tart

Ingredients for 6 servings

Dough:

2 tbsps extra-virgin olive oil
1 shallot, minced
2 medium potatoes, peeled and thinly sliced
2 cups (500 ml) hot vegetable broth
salt and pepper
3 oz (80 g) bacon, diced
1 egg, lightly beaten
3 tbsps grated Parmesan cheese
9 oz (250 g) puff pastry (see page 385)
1 tbsp sesame seeds

Preheat the oven to 400°F (200°C or Gas Mark 6). Heat the olive oil in a frying pan and add the shallot. Sauté and add the potatoes. Sauté the potatoes briefly and add the broth. Cover and cook over medium-low heat until tender. Puree the mixture and season to taste with salt and pepper. Render the bacon in a frying pan with a little olive oil until crunchy. Add the bacon to the potato puree and stir in the egg, Parmesan and a pinch of pepper. Line the puff pastry in a baking dish lined with parchment paper. Pierce the dough with a fork and spread in the potato mixture. Sprinkle over the sesame seeds and bake for 35 minutes. Let cool slightly and serve.

For a rich variation, brown some sausage and add it to the potato puree along with the bacon.

Preparation time **20 minutes**
Cooking time **45 minutes**
Level **easy**
Wine **Prosecco di Conegliano e Valdobbiadene Extra Dry**

quiche lorraine

Ingredients for 4 servings

Dough:

1 tab of butter

1 tbsp all-purpose flour

12½ oz (350 g) pâte brisée dough (see page 386)

3 eggs, **7** tbsps heavy cream

7 tbsps milk, salt and pepper, nutmeg

2 oz (50 g) Emmenthal cheese, sliced into matchsticks

12½ oz (350 g) smoked pancetta, sliced into matchsticks

Preheat the oven to 350°F (180°C or Gas Mark 4).
Butter and flour a high-rimmed baking dish.
Roll out the dough and use it to line the prepared dish.
Pierce the dough with a fork.
Beat the eggs with the cream and milk and season with a pinch of salt and abundant freshly ground pepper.
Add a grating of nutmeg, the cheese and pancetta.
Pour the batter over the dough and bake for 45 minutes.
Remove from the oven, let cool slightly and serve.

Aromatic herbs may be added to the batter when they are in season in the spring and summer. In the winter try adding a leek or yellow onion sautéed in a little butter.

Preparation time **20 minutes**
Cooking time **45 minutes**
Level **easy**
Wine **Alto Adige Santa Maddalena**

vesuvian strudel

Ingredients for 4 servings

Dough:

9 oz (250 g) puff pastry (see page 385)

7 oz (200 g) mild provolone cheese, sliced

1 large tomato, peeled and diced

2 tbsps (1 oz or 25 g) capers, minced

4 anchovy fillets in salt, rinsed and minced

3 tbsps (2 oz or 50 g) pitted green olives, minced

1 tsp dried oregano

salt and pepper

Preheat the oven to 375°F (190°C or Gas Mark 5). Roll the pastry out thinly on a floured work surface. Cover the pastry with a layer of provolone slices, top with the diced tomatoes, capers, olives and anchovies. Sprinkle over the oregano and roll up the strudel. Seal the top edge and both ends and place on a baking sheet lined with parchment paper.
Bake for about 30 minutes.
Remove from the oven and let cool slightly before serving.

Provolone is an Italian cheese originally from the south of the country, but now produced in the north and in North America. It is made from whole cow's milk and can be shaped like a cylinder or a pear. Its flavor depends on how long it has been aged.

Preparation time **30 minutes**
Cooking time **30 minutes**
Level **easy**
Wine **Greco di Tufo**

radicchio and winter squash tart

Ingredients for 6 servings

Puff pastry dough:

3/4 cup plus 1 tbsp (3½ oz or 100 g) all-purpose flour

9 tbsps (4½ oz or 125 g) margarine

3 tbsps (50 ml) water, salt

Pâte brisée dough:

1⅔ cups (200 g) all-purpose flour

2 tbsps (30 ml) water

6 tbsps (3 oz or 80 g) butter, salt

Filling:

3 tbsps extra virgin olive oil

1 onion, thinly sliced

1/2 pumpkin or other winter squash, peeled, deseeded and diced

1/2 head of radicchio, shredded

2 cups (9 oz or 250 g) peas

1 egg, salt and pepper

2 tbsps sesame seeds

1 tbsp sunflower seeds

Prepare the puff pastry and the pâte brisée according to the recipes on pages 385 and 386. Roll out both of the doughs on a lightly floured work surface. Preheat the oven to 375°F (190°C or Gas Mark 5). Heat 1 tablespoon olive oil in a large frying pan and add half of the onion and all of the pumpkin. Add 4 tablespoons of water and cook for 10 minutes. Heat the remaining olive oil in another frying pan and add the remaining onion and the radicchio. Let cook for a few minutes until soft. Meanwhile, blanch the peas in boiling salted water for 2 minutes. Puree the pumpkin in a food processor and then mix in the peas and radicchio. Add the egg and mix well to combine, then season to taste with salt and pepper. Line a tart tin with the pâte brisée, fill with the pumpkin mixture and cover with puff pastry. Score the pastry surface, brush with oil and sprinkle with sesame and sunflower seeds. Bake for 30 minutes and serve warm.

Preparation time **25 minutes**
Cooking time **45 minutes**
Level **medium**
Wine **Lugana**

carrot, escarole and zucchini tart

Ingredients for 4 servings

Dough:

3 tbsps extra-virgin olive oil

2 garlic cloves

1 head of escarole, coarsely chopped

2 carrots, diced, **3** zucchini, diced

salt and pepper

2 thyme sprigs, leaves only

9 oz (250 g) pâte brisée dough (see page 386)

2 tbsps poppy seeds

Preheat the oven to 350°F (180°C or Gas Mark 4).
Heat the half of the olive oil in a large frying pan and brown 1 garlic clove. Add the escarole and sauté for 5 minutes over medium heat. Season to taste with salt and pepper.
In another frying pan heat the remaining olive oil and brown the other garlic clove. Remove the garlic and add the carrots and zucchini. Season with salt and the thyme leaves and remove from heat when tender.
Mix all of the vegetables together.
Roll out the pâte brisée dough and place it in a baking dish. Cover with the sautéed vegetables and smooth with a spatula. Sprinkle over the poppy seeds and bake for 30 minutes. Remove from the oven and serve hot.

Try making this tart with the following filling: sauté 1 lb (500 g) escarole with 1 sliced red onion and 2 tablespoons extra-virgin olive oil for 10 minutes. Add a handful of pine nuts, pitted black olives and 5-6 capers. Season with salt and pepper and pour into a tart pan lined with pâte brisée. Bake for 25 minutes.

Preparation time **15 minutes**
Cooking time **40 minutes**
Level **easy**
Wine **Ischia Bianco**

asparagus bread

Ingredients for 4 servings

Dough:

9 oz (250 g) pâte brisée (see page 386)

1 tab of butter

1⅓ cups plus 1 tbsp (180 g) all-purpose flour

8 large asparagus spears

salt and pepper

3 eggs, **7** tbsps milk

1 tsp baking powder

6 tbsps extra-virgin olive oil

2½ oz (100 g) goat's milk cheese, chopped

2 tbsps grated Gruyère cheese

Preheat the oven to 375°F (190°C or Gas Mark 5). Butter and flour a loaf pan and line it with the pâte brisée. Bake for 12 minutes. Remove from the oven and turn the oven down to 350°F (180°C or Gas Mark 4). Blanch the asparagus spears in lightly salted water. Beat the eggs, milk, salt and pepper together in a mixing bowl. Sift in the remaining flour and baking powder and stir in the olive oil, goat's cheese and Gruyère. Pour half the batter into the baked brisée crust, top with half of the asparagus and pour in the remaining batter. Place the remaining asparagus on top of the batter and bake for 45 minutes.
Remove from the oven, let cool and unmold.
Serve the bread warm.

⌐ Other spring vegetables like peas, zucchini, green beans or snow peas may be used in place of the asparagus.

Preparation time **30 minutes**
Cooking time **50 minutes**
Level **easy**
Wine **Alto Adige Gewürztraminer**

emmenthal and tomato tart

Ingredients for 6 servings

Dough:
9 oz (250 g) all-purpose flour
9 tbsps (4½ oz or 125 g) butter
1/2 tsp salt

Filling:
2 medium tomatoes
7 slices of bread
1 onion, minced
1 bunch of chives, minced
7 oz (200 g) Emmenthal cheese, sliced
3 eggs
1 cup (250 ml) heavy cream
pepper
1 tsp sesame seeds

Mix together the flour, butter and salt and add enough water to form a smooth dough. Roll out the dough and place it in a buttered baking dish. Refrigerate for 30 minutes.
Preheat the oven to 400°F (200°C or Gas Mark 6). Blanch the tomatoes in boiling water for a few seconds. Drain, remove the skin and slice.
Layer the bread, tomatoes, onion, chives and finally the cheese over the tart crust.
Beat the eggs with the cream and season with pepper. Pour the mixture over the tart and sprinkle with sesame seeds. Bake for 30 minutes.
Remove from the oven and let cool slightly before serving.

Asiago or fontina cheese may used in place of the Emmenthal in this recipe.

Preparation time **15 minutes**
Cooking time **30 minutes**
Level **easy**
Wine **Ribolla Gialla**

potato and porcini strudel

Ingredients for 4 servings

Dough:
1¼ tsp (10 g) active dry yeast, salt
2⅓ cups plus 1 tbsp (10½ oz or 300 g) all-purpose flour

Filling:
2 medium potatoes, salt and pepper
4 tbsps extra-virgin olive oil
2 garlic cloves, smashed, 2 eggs
7 oz (200 g) fresh porcini mushrooms, thinly sliced
3 tbsps grated Parmesan cheese
1 spring onion, thinly sliced
1 thyme sprig, leaves only

Though more commonly found dried, fresh porcini mushrooms are a great delicacy and very popular in Italy in the autumn and winter months. They must be carefully cleaned before using; wipe the caps with a damp paper towel and trim off the earthy part of the stalk.

Preheat the oven to 375°F (190°C or Gas Mark 5). Dissolve the yeast in a little warm water. Mound the flour on a work surface and make a well in the center. Pour the yeast mixture into the well, add a pinch of salt and mix, adding enough water to form a smooth dough. Cover and let rest for 20 minutes. Place the potatoes in a saucepan of cold water and bring to a boil. Cook until tender, then drain, peel and mash. Heat 2 tablespoons olive oil in a frying pan and brown the garlic cloves. Add the porcini mushrooms and sauté for a few minutes.
Add the mushrooms to the potatoes and mix in 1 egg, the Parmesan, spring onion and thyme leaves and season with pinches of salt and pepper. Roll out the dough into a thin rectangular sheet. Place the potato filling in the center of the dough and spread into a long strip. Roll up the dough like a jelly roll and pinch the ends closed to seal. Transfer to a baking sheet and let rise for 10-15 minutes. Beat the remaining egg and brush the strudel with it. Bake for 25-30 minutes. Remove from the oven and serve in thick slices with a green salad if desired.

Preparation time **1 hour**
Cooking time **1 hour 30 minutes**
Level **easy**
Wine **Alto Adige Santa Maddalena**

salt cod and broccoli pie

Ingredients for 4 servings

Dough:

1 lb 1½ oz (500 g) puff pastry (see page 385)

1 egg

Filling:

14 oz (400 g) salt cod, soaked and rinsed

1/2 onion, minced

4 tbsps extra-virgin olive oil

2 tomatoes, diced

salt and pepper

1 large head of broccoli, cut into florets

2 eggs

7 tbsps grated Parmesan cheese

Preheat the oven to 375°F (190°C or Gas Mark 5). Remove the skin from the salt cod and break the fish into pieces.
Sauté the onion in the olive oil and add the cod. Add the tomatoes and season with pinches of salt and pepper. Cover and cook for about 15 minutes.
Blanch the broccoli in salted water until just tender. Drain, coarsely chop and add to the fish sauté. Remove from the heat and stir in 1 egg and the Parmesan cheese.
Use a sheet of puff pastry to line a 10-inch (24 cm) round tart pan. Pour in the filling and top with the remaining puff pastry. Pinch the edges to seal and brush the top with the remaining egg, lightly beaten.
Pierce the top of the tart with a toothpick and bake for 30-35 minutes or until the top is golden-brown. Serve hot or warm.

For a more mild flavor, substitute the broccoli with 2-3 boiled, peeled and mashed potatoes.

Preparation time **20 minutes**
Cooking time **45 minutes**
Level **easy**
Wine **Friuli Vitovska**

cardoon and salt cod strudel with tomato sauce

Ingredients for 6 servings

Dough:

1 lb 1½ oz (500 g) puff pastry (see page 385)

1 egg, lightly beaten

Filling:

7 oz (200 g) boiled cardoons, julienned

9 oz (250 g) salt cod fillets, soaked and rinsed

3½ oz (100 g) mozzarella, diced

Sauce:

3 tbsps extra-virgin olive oil

1 garlic clove, **5** basil leaves

2/3 cup (3½ oz or 100 g) cherry tomatoes, lightly smashed

salt and pepper

3/4 cup (200 ml) vegetable broth

Preheat the oven to 400°F (200°C or Gas Mark 6). Roll out the puff pastry on a lightly floured kitchen towel. Top with the cardoons, crumbled salt cod and mozzarella. Roll up the dough like a jelly roll and pinch the ends closed. Transfer to a baking sheet, using the towel to help. Brush the strudel with the beaten egg and make diagonal incisions along the top. Bake for 10 minutes, reduce the oven temperature to 350°F (180°C or Gas Mark 4) and continue baking for another 30 minutes. Meanwhile, make the sauce. Heat the olive oil in a frying pan and add the whole garlic clove, basil leaves and tomatoes. Season to taste with salt and pepper and thin with some of the vegetable broth. Cook for 10 minutes, or until the sauce reaches the desired consistency, adding more vegetable broth as necessary. Remove from heat and strain the sauce. Place a spoonful of sauce on each serving plate and top with a slice of strudel. Serve immediately.

Preparation time **20 minutes**
Cooking time **40 minutes**
Level **easy**
Wine **Inzolia**

spinach and swiss chard savory tart

Ingredients for 6 servings

Dough:

1 2/3 cups (7 oz or 200 g) all-purpose flour
1/2 cup (120 ml) water
3 tbsps extra-virgin olive oil
salt and pepper
7 oz (200 g) spinach
7 oz (200 g) Swiss chard
1 garlic clove, smashed
4 tbsps grated Parmesan cheese
nutmeg

Preheat the oven to 350°F (180°C or Gas Mark 4). Mix together the flour, water, 2 tablespoons of olive oil and a pinch of salt to form a thick dough.
Blanch the spinach and Swiss chard separately in salted water. Drain, squeeze out the excess water and sauté together in a large frying pan with 1 tablespoon of olive oil and the smashed garlic clove. Transfer the greens to a mixing bowl and add the Parmesan and pinches of salt and pepper and season to taste with freshly grated nutmeg.
Divide the dough in half. Roll the dough into 2 thin rounds and line 1 round into an oiled tart tin. Spread the spinach mixture over the dough and cover with the remaining dough round. Pierce the top with a fork and cook for 30-35 minutes, or until the top is golden brown.

Preparation time **30 minutes**
Cooking time **45 minutes**
Level **medium**
Wine **Ribolla Gialla**

savory pear and parmesan strudel

Ingredients for 6 servings

Dough:

9 oz (250 g) puff pastry or phyllo dough (see page 385)

5½ oz (150 g) unaged pancetta, thinly sliced

1/3 cup (1½ oz or 50 g) walnuts, coarsely chopped

2 pears, peeled and sliced

2/3 cup (2 oz or 60 g) Parmesan cheese shavings

salt and pepper

2 tbsps extra-virgin olive oil

1 tbsp melted butter, fennel seeds

Preheat the oven to 350°F (180°C or Gas Mark 4).
Roll out the puff pastry. Cover with slightly overlapping slices of pancetta and the walnuts.
Place the pear slices on top and sprinkle with Parmesan cheese shavings, salt and pepper. Drizzle with olive oil and roll up the pastry.
Pinch outside edges shut. Brush with melted butter and sprinkle fennel seeds over the top.
Bake for 20 minutes and serve warm.

⌐Parmesan and pears are a great combination. An Italian proverb says "Don't let the peasant know how good cheese is with pears."

Preparation time **15 minutes**
Cooking time **20 minutes**
Level **easy**
Wine **Metodo Trento Talento Brut**

savory zucchini, tomato and fontina tart

Ingredients for 4 servings

Pâte brisée:

2⅓ plus 1 tbsp (10½ oz or 300 g) all-purpose flour

9 tbsps (4½ oz or 125 g) butter or margarine

3 tbsps (50 ml) water

salt

Filling:

2 zucchini, diced

2 tbsps extra-virgin olive oil

salt and pepper

12 cherry tomatoes, quartered

10½ oz (300 g) fontina cheese, diced

Preheat the oven to 350°F (180°C or Gas Mark 4). Prepare the dough following the recipe on page 386. Sauté the zucchini in the olive oil for 5 minutes. Season to taste with salt and pepper and set aside. Roll out the pâte brisée and use it to line a tart tin. Top with the sautéed zucchini, cherry tomatoes and fontina. Bake for 20 minutes and serve hot.

Enrich this tart by adding 1 diced eggplant and 1 diced bell pepper to the zucchini sauté.

Preparation time **30 minutes**
Cooking time **25 minutes**
Level **easy**
Wine **Roero Arneis**

eggplant, mozzarella and egg tart

Ingredients for 6 servings

Pâte brisée:

2⅓ plus 1 tbsp (10½ oz or 300 g) all-purpose flour

9 tbsps (4½ oz or 125 g) butter or margarine

3 tbsps (50 ml) water

salt

Filling:

1 eggplant, sliced

salt and pepper

2 whole mozzarellas, diced

1 hard-boiled egg, peeled

extra-virgin olive oil

Prepare the dough following the recipe on page 386. Preheat the oven to 300°F (150°C or Gas Mark 2). Salt the eggplant slices and place in a colander with a plate on top weighed down with some cans. Let sit for 30 minutes, then rinse and drain. Place the eggplant on a baking sheet and bake for 10 minutes. Remove from the oven and puree with half of the mozzarella. Season to taste with salt and pepper. Raise the oven temperature to 350°F (180°C or Gas Mark 4). Roll out half of the dough and use it to line a round tart tin. Place the hard-boiled egg in the center of the dough and sprinkle the remaining mozzarella around it. Top with the eggplant puree. Roll out the remaining dough and cover the tart with it.
Pinch the edges to seal and pierce the top with a fork. Brush the tart with olive oil and bake for 20 minutes.

The eggplant may be substituted with 1 bunch of asparagus, blanched and pureed.

Preparation time **25 minutes**
Cooking time **30 minutes**
Level **easy**
Wine **Alto Adige Sauvignon**

beyond sandwiches

Pizza

mediterranean crostoni

Ingredients for 4 servings
4 large taralli or toasted bread slices
white wine vinegar
4 tomatoes, sliced
2 celery stalks, chopped
1 bell pepper, sliced
1 cucumber, sliced
2 hard-boiled eggs, peeled and sliced
1/2 cup (2 oz or 50 g) pitted black and green olives
3½ oz (100 g) anchovies in oil, drained
2 garlic cloves, minced
salt, oregano
6 tbsps extra-virgin olive oil

Brush a little vinegar over the taralli and pat dry with a paper towel.
Place them on a serving plate and top with the tomato, celery, bell pepper and cucumber. Place the eggs on top of the toasts. Add the olives, anchovies and garlic. Season with a pinch of salt, sprinkle with oregano and drizzle with olive oil. Let sit in a cool place for at least 30 minutes before serving.

beyond sandwiches

Taralli are crunchy, savory crackers from Puglia, made with olive oil.

Preparation time **20 minutes**
Cooking time **5 minutes**
Level **easy**
Wine **Sicilia Chardonnay**

mini panini with speck and artichokes

Ingredients for 4 servings

8 small dinner rolls

8 slices of speck

8 whole artichokes in oil, drained and sliced

5½ oz (150 g) fontina cheese, sliced into matchsticks

Slice the rolls in half. Drain the artichokes and slice them. Make sandwiches by layering a few artichoke slices, 1 slice of speck and a few pieces of cheese on the bottom halves of the rolls. Close the sandwiches with the top halves and secure with a toothpick.

The artichokes may be substituted with chopped arugula dressed with salt, pepper and olive oil.

Preparation time **5 minutes**
Level **easy**
Wine **Lago di Caldaro Schiava**

crostini with prosciutto and mushrooms

Ingredients for 4-6 servings

4 tbsps (2 oz or 60 g) butter

1¼ cups (3½ oz or 100 g) sliced mushrooms

salt

1 bunch of parsley, minced

3 slices of white bread, halved

2-3½ oz (100g) balls of mozzarella, diced

6 slices of prosciutto

Preheat the oven to 350°F (180°C or Gas Mark 4). Melt half the butter and sauté the mushrooms for 15 minutes. Season to taste with salt and sprinkle over the parsley, reserving some for garnish.
Melt the remaining butter in a frying pan and brown the bread slices on both sides. Place the bread on a baking sheet. Top with the mozzarella and prosciutto. Add a spoonful of mushrooms to each crostini and bake until the cheese is completely melted.
Serve the crostini hot, sprinkled with parsley.

The mushrooms may be substituted with thinly sliced zucchini sautéed with garlic.

Preparation time **15 minutes**
Cooking time **20 minutes**
Level **easy**
Wine **Aprilia Trebbiano**

mozzarella in carrozza

Ingredients for 4 servings
8 slices of sandwich bread
1 whole mozzarella, sliced
all-purpose flour
2 eggs
salt
extra-virgin olive oil

Trim the crusts off the bread. Top half the bread slices with mozzarella, and close with the other half. Dust with flour and brush the edges with a little water. Press down to seal.
Beat the eggs with a pinch of salt and soak the sandwiches into the egg mixture for a few minutes. Heat abundant olive oil in a deep frying pan and fry the sandwiches until golden-brown on both sides. Remove from the pan using a slotted spoon and place on paper towels to dry. Serve immediately.

beyond sandwiches

Enrich this recipe by adding a slice of ham to each sandwich.

Preparation time **15 minutes**
Cooking time **10 minutes**
Level **medium**
Wine **Ischia Bianco**

zucchini and smoked salmon panini

Ingredients for 4 servings

2 zucchini, sliced
salt and pepper
6 tbsps extra-virgin olive oil
15 basil leaves
4 small multigrain rolls
9 oz (250 g) smoked salmon, sliced

Season the zucchini with pinches of salt and pepper and drizzle with 2 tablespoons of olive oil.
Heat a grill pan and grill the zucchini for 2-3 minutes.
Puree the basil with the remaining olive oil.
Slice the rolls in half and spread the basil oil on each side.
Top with 1 grilled zucchini slice and half a slice of salmon.
Place the tops on the sandwiches and secure with a toothpick if necessary.
Let sit for a few minutes before serving.

Cuisinart or food processor are names for electric kitchen appliances that are fitted with a metal or plastic blade and are used to chop, mix, puree and blend.

Preparation time **10 minutes**
Cooking time **5 minutes**
Level **easy**
Wine **Metodo Classico Franciacorta Brut**

fried spinach ravioli

Ingredients for 4 servings

Dough:

1 lb 1½ oz (500 g) all-purpose flour

5 tbsps extra-virgin olive oil

7 tbsps milk

1 tsp baking powder

salt

Filling:

1 large tab of butter

1 lb 1½ oz (500 g) spinach, chopped

3½ oz (100 g) caciotta cheese (see note), diced

extra-virgin olive oil

Mound the flour on a work surface and make a well in the center. Pour in the olive oil and milk and add a pinch of salt and the baking powder. Mix to form a rough dough and then knead until smooth.
Cover with a kitchen towel and let rest for 30 minutes. Divide the dough into small portions and roll out each one into a circle. Heat the butter in a frying pan and add the spinach. Season to taste with salt and cook until tender. Place a spoonful of spinach in the center of each dough round and top with a few cubes of cheese.
Fold the rounds in half to form half-moon shapes and seal the edges. Heat abundant olive oil in a large frying pan and fry the ravioli until both sides are golden-brown. Drain using a slotted spoon and serve hot.

Caciotta cheese may be substituted with diced mozzarella or fontina.

Preparation time **40 minutes**
Cooking time **30 minutes**
Level **easy**
Wine **Verdicchio dei Castelli di Jesi Spumante**

crispy piadinas with crab salad

Ingredients for 4 servings

Piadinas:

4 cups (1 lb 1½ oz or 500 g) all-purpose flour

3 tbsps lard

water, salt

Filling:

7 oz (200 g) crab meat

3 tbsps extra-virgin olive oil

salt and pepper

parsley, minced

juice of ½ lemon

1 head of green lettuce (iceberg or curly leaf), shredded

5 oz (150 g) grilled eggplant in oil, drained and patted dry

10 cherry tomatoes, quartered

Preheat the oven to 350°F (180°C or Gas Mark 4).
Make the piadinas following the recipe on page 387.
Drain the crab meat and mix with the olive oil, salt, pepper and parsley. Add the lemon juice. Toss with the shredded lettuce. Add the eggplant and tomatoes.
Toast the piadinas in the oven for 7 minutes, until crunchy.
Serve the salad on top of the piadinas and drizzle with extra olive oil if desired.

Preparation time **20 minutes**
Cooking time **10 minutes**
Level **easy**
Wine **Trebbiano di Romagna**

panini with bresaola, cherry tomatoes and parmesan

Ingredients for 4 servings
10 cherry tomatoes, halved
salt
2 tbsps extra-virgin olive oil
4 small whole-wheat rolls
12 slices of bresaola
1½ oz (40 g) Parmesan, shaved

Season the cherry tomatoes to taste with salt and drizzle with the olive oil. Slice the rolls in half horizontally and fill them with 3 slices of bresaola, a few cherry tomatoes and a few Parmesan shavings.
Place the tops on the sandwiches and secure with a toothpick if necessary. Serve with a garnish of a few lettuce leaves if desired.

If bresaola is unavailable, use slices of prosciutto instead and substitute the Parmesan with the same quantity of semi-aged pecorino cheese.

Preparation time **5 minutes**
Level **easy**
Wine **Valcalepio Bianco**

baked ravioli

Ingredients for 4 servings
Dough:
1/2 cup (3½ oz or 100 g) lard
4 cups (1 lb 1½ oz or 500 g) all-purpose flour
Filling:
9 oz (250 g) pork, chopped
9 oz (250 g) beef, chopped
2 oz (50 g) sausage meat
3½ oz (100 g) pitted black olives
3½ oz (100 g) sun-dried tomatoes, chopped
1 garlic clove, minced, parsley, minced
extra-virgin olive oil, salt and pepper

Mix together the meat and crumble in the sausage. Add the olives, sun-dried tomatoes, garlic and parsley. Season with pinches of salt and pepper and drizzle with olive oil. Marinate for 3 hours.
Preheat the oven to 350°F (180°C or Gas Mark 4). Melt the lard in a small pan over low heat. Mound the flour on a work surface and make a well in the center. Pour in the lard and add enough water to form a smooth dough. Let rest for at least 30 minutes.
Roll out the dough and cut out small rounds using a cookie cutter. Place spoonfuls of the meat mixture and a little of its liquid on half of the dough rounds. Top with the remaining dough rounds and pinch the edges to seal. Transfer the to an oiled baking sheet and bake for about 40 minutes. Serve warm.

Marinades help to preserve and soften the meat. They are usually made with wine, vinegar and a mix of onions, carrots, celery, and shallots. Seasonings can include fresh herbs like bay and thyme and spices like pepper, juniper berries and cloves.

Preparation time **20 minutes**
Cooking time **40 minutes**
Level **easy**
Wine **Carignano del Sulcis Rosso**

sweet and sour crostini

Ingredients for 4 servings
1 lb (500 g) prosciutto
1 tsp sugar
1/2 tsp ground cinnamon
6 tbps white wine vinegar
1 loaf brioche bread, sliced

Chop the prosciutto into small pieces and then mince it using a sharp chef's knife. Brown the prosciutto in a non-stick pan. Do not use any oil as the fat from the prosciutto will render and create enough moisture. Dissolve the sugar and cinnamon in the vinegar. When the prosciutto begins to color, add the vinegar mixture. Crumble over 5 slices of brioche bread and simmer until the sauce becomes concentrated.
Slice the remaining bread and toast it under the broiler. Spread the prosciutto sauce over the bread and serve the crostini immediately.

Preparation time **15 minutes**
Cooking time **15 minutes**
Level **easy**
Wine **Sangiovese di Romagna**

fried bread

Ingredients for 4 servings
1 lb (500 g) dry bread, thickly sliced
1 cup (250 ml) milk
3 eggs
salt
1 bunch of parsley, minced
2 tbsps all-purpose flour
sunflower oil

Remove the crusts from the bread slices and soak them briefly in the milk. Remove before the bread begins to lose its shape. Beat the eggs with a pinch of salt and the parsley. Dust the bread with the flour and dip in the egg mixture, coating the bread thoroughly.
Heat abundant sunflower oil in a frying pan and fry the bread until golden on both sides. Drain on paper towels and serve hot.

beyond sandwiches

⌐ Fried bread can be served as an appetizer or to accompany soups or vegetable stews.

Preparation time **10 minutes**
Cooking time **5 minutes**
Level **easy**
Wine **Nasco di Cagliari**

tigelle

Ingredients for 4 servings

Tigelle:

4¼ tsps (25 g) active dry yeast

4¾ cups (1 lb 5 oz or 600 g) all-purpose flour

4 tbsps lard, salt

3/4 cup plus 2 tbsps (200 ml) heavy cream

Spread:

7 oz (200 g) lardo (cured lard), minced

1 garlic clove, minced

rosemary, minced

2 tbsps grated Parmesan cheese

pepper

Dissolve the yeast in a little warm water. Mix the flour with the yeast mixture, lard and a pinch of salt, then add the cream and knead to form a smooth dough.
Let rest for 1 hour.
Once the dough has rested, form cylinders of around 1 inch (2½ cm) in diameter, then tear off pieces of the same length. Form them into balls, then flatten them, creating a hollow on one side.
Let them rest for 30 minutes on a clean kitchen towel.
Preheat the oven to 350°F (180°C or Gas Mark 4).
Once the tigelle have rested, press them out to form circles 4 inches (10 cm) in diameter and ¼-inch (½ cm) thick. Bake in the oven until golden.
Meanwhile make the spread by grinding the lardo with the garlic, a little rosemary, the Parmesan and a pinch of pepper in a mortar and pestle.
Serve the tigelle hot, opened and filled with the spread or with a selection of cured meats and soft cheeses.

This is the version from Modena of a typical Emilian bread. Traditionally tigelle were cooked between hot stones or terracotta tiles.

Preparation time **25 minutes**
Cooking time **15 minutes**
Level **easy**
Wine **Lambrusco Salamino di Santa Croce**

farro crêpes with onions and olives

Ingredients for 4 servings

Crêpes:

2 eggs
2 cups (500 ml) milk
1 cup (4½ oz or 130 g) farro (emmer) flour
½ cup plus 1 tbsp (70 g) all-purpose flour
salt and pepper
1 tbsp extra-virgin olive oil

Filling:

2 large yellow onions, thinly sliced
2 tbsps sunflower oil
2 tbsps pitted black olives, chopped
1 bunch of marjoram, destemmed

Beat the eggs with the milk and add the farro and all-purpose flour a little at a time. Mix to form a fluid batter without any lumps. Let rest for 20 minutes and season with pinches of salt and pepper.

Heat a small non-stick frying pan or crêpe pan, brush with a little olive oil and pour in a little batter. Turn the pan so that the batter covers it in an even layer. Flip and cook until golden brown. Make as many small crêpes as the batter will allow.

Cook the onions in a frying pan with the sunflower oil and 1 tablespoon of water. Stir frequently and remove from the heat when the onions are translucent and beginning to brown. Stir together the olives and the onions and sprinkle over the marjoram leaves. Fill the crêpes with the onion mixture and fold in half and then in half again to form a triangle. Serve immediately.

Farro is also known as emmer wheat, and is an ancient grain with many nutritional benefits.

Preparation time **15 minutes**
Cooking time **10 minutes**
Level **easy**
Wine **Prosecco di Conegliano e Valdobbiadene Extra Dry**

asparagus fritters

Ingredients for 4 servings
3/4 tsp (6 g) active dry yeast
1/3 cup (80 ml) warm water
salt and freshly ground black pepper
1 tbsp extra-virgin olive oil
1¼ cups (5½ oz or 150 g) all-purpose flour
6 thin asparagus spears
1 thyme sprig, leaves only
sunflower oil

Dissolve the yeast in the warm water and let sit until it dissolves completely. Add a large pinch of salt and the olive oil. Sift the flour onto a work surface and form a well in the center. Pour in the yeast mixture and stir to form a dough. Knead the dough until smooth, cover with a damp cloth and let rest for 30 minutes.
Snap off the hard base of the asparagus spears, and peel the lower half with a vegetable peeler.
Blanch the asparagus in boiling salted water for about 3 minutes, drain and immerse in cold water. Once cooled, thinly slice into rounds. Knead the risen dough and mix in a pinch of pepper, the thyme leaves and the asparagus until evenly incorporated. Heat the sunflower oil and fry spoonfuls of the dough. Drain on paper towels, sprinkle with salt and serve immediately.

For lighter fritters, substitute this dough with a thick batter made by whisking together flour and sparkling water. Add the asparagus and thyme to the batter and proceed with the recipe.

Preparation time **10 minutes**
Cooking time **10 minutes**
Level **easy**
Wine **Colli di Conegliano Verdiso**

chickpea crêpes with green salad

Ingredients for 4 servings

1 cup (3½ oz or 100 g) chickpea flour
3/4 cup (3½ oz or 100 g) all-purpose flour
5 tbsps extra-virgin olive oil
salt
2 cups (500 ml) milk
1 tbsp melted butter
1 head butter lettuce, shredded
juice from ½ lemon

Sift the flours into a mixing bowl and add 3 tablespoons of olive oil and a pinch of salt. Whisk in the milk and stir in the melted butter. Mix until smooth and let rest for 20 minutes.
Heat a non-stick pan or crêpe pan and pour in a ladleful of batter. Turn the pan to coat it with an even layer of batter. Flip the crêpe and cook until it begins to color.
Continue making the crêpes until the batter is finished. Whisk together the lemon juice and the remaining olive oil with a little salt until emulsified. Dress the lettuce with the dressing and serve with the warm chickpea crêpes.

The best way to melt butter is in a double boiler, a container or small pan set over another pan of gently boiling water. However it can also be melted in the microwave.

Preparation time **20 minutes**
Cooking time **30 minutes**
Level **easy**
Wine **Prosecco di Conegliano e Valdobbiadene Brut**

walnut and pecorino rolls

Ingredients for 4 servings

- **1** lb (500 g) walnuts
- **4** tsps (30 g) active dry yeast
- **2** cups (500 ml) warm milk
- **8** cups (2 lb 3 oz or 1 kg) all-purpose flour
- **1** tsp salt
- **1** tsp ground pepper
- **7** tbsps extra-virgin olive oil
- **1/3** cup plus 1 tbsp (3 oz or 80 g) lard
- **7** oz (200 g) pecorino cheese, cubed
- **1½** tbsps butter
- **1** egg, lightly beaten

Pour boiling water over the walnuts and let them soak for 5 minutes. Drain and transfer to a kitchen towel. Rub the nuts until the skins fall off.
Dissolve the yeast in 1½ cups (400 ml) warm milk. Mound half of the flour on a work surface and add the yeast mixture. Mix to combine and then knead to form a smooth dough. Cover with a towel and let rise for 30 minutes. Pour the rest of the flour into a mixing bowl and add the salt, pepper, remaining milk, olive oil and lard. Mix and then add the risen dough and knead vigorously until smooth. Cover and let rise for 30 minutes. Divide the dough into small portions and place a cube of pecorino and a few walnut halves on each portion. Push the cheese and walnuts into the dough and let rise for another 2 hours.
Preheat the oven to 400°F (200°C or Gas Mark 6). Transfer the rolls to a buttered baking sheet and brush with the beaten egg. Bake for 30 minutes and serve warm.

These rolls come from the Marche region in central Italy. They can be served with salami and other cured meats.

Preparation time **45 minutes**
Cooking time **30 minutes**
Level **medium**
Wine **Verdicchio di Matelica Spumante**

flatbreads stuffed with potatoes and pancetta

Ingredients for 4 servings

Dough:

1 cup (4½ oz or 125 g) all-purpose flour

1 tsp baking soda

Filling:

1 large potato (about 7 oz or 200 g)

salt and pepper

3½ oz (100 g) pancetta, diced

1/3 cup (1 oz or 30 g) grated Parmesan cheese

mixed herbs (rosemary, thyme, sage), minced

Mix together the flour and baking soda and add enough water to make a smooth dough. Roll the dough into a ball, cover and let rest.
Meanwhile, boil the potato in salted water until tender. Drain, peel and mash. Render the pancetta and add it to the potatoes, along with the drippings.
Stir in the Parmesan and season to taste with salt and pepper and the minced herbs. Stir the filling until the pancetta and herbs are evenly distributed throughout. Roll out the dough and cut out circles using a round cookie cutter. Place a spoonful of filling on each round and fold in half. Cook the stuffed flatbreads in a hot non-stick pan or on a griddle until they begin to brown. Serve hot.

Cookie cutters come in many shapes and sizes and have various uses in the kitchen. They are most often used to cut dough into specific shapes, but they can also be used as molds when plating dishes.

Preparation time **40 minutes**
Cooking time **20 minutes**
Level **easy**
Wine **Colli Bolognesi Barbera Vivace**

ricotta and prosciutto panzerotti

Ingredients for 4 servings

Dough:
2⅓ cups plus 1 tbsp (10½ oz or 300 g) all-purpose flour
1 tbsp lard, salt

Filling:
1 egg, 1 bunch of parsley, minced
salt and pepper, sunflower oil
3½ oz (100 g) ricotta
2 oz (50 g) mozzarella, diced
5 tbsps grated Parmesan cheese
3½ oz (100 g) prosciutto, thinly sliced and diced

Mound the flour on a work surface and make a well at the center. Place the lard and a pinch of salt in the center and add enough water to form a smooth dough. Knead well and let rise for 1 hour.
Mix together the egg, parsley and a pinch of salt. Beat the ricotta until smooth and stir in the egg mixture. Stir in the mozzarella, Parmesan and prosciutto. Roll out the dough into a thin sheet and place spoonfuls of filling at 2-inch (5 cm) intervals along one side of the dough. Fold the dough over and press down around the filling to seal. Use a round cookie cutter or ravioli cutter to cut out the panzerotti. Heat abundant sunflower oil in a pot and fry the panzerotti. Drain with a slotted spoon as soon as they are lightly browned on both sides. Dry on paper towels and serve hot.

⌐ Add a little chopped basil to the panzerotti filling for added flavor. The prosciutto may be substituted with the same quantity of ham if desired.

Preparation time **40 minutes**
Cooking time **20 minutes**
Level **easy**
Wine **Greco di Tufo**

mini potato focaccias with lardo and rosemary

Ingredients for 4 servings

Dough:

1 large potato (about 7 oz or 200 g)

1¾ tsps (12 g) active dry yeast, salt

3/4 cup plus 1 tbsp (200 ml) water

3¼ cups (14 oz or 400 g) all-purpose flour

3 tbsps extra-virgin olive oil

Topping:

7 oz (200 g) lardo (cured lard), thinly sliced

1 rosemary sprig, minced

5 tbsps extra-virgin olive oil all-purpose flour

1/2 tsp coarse sea salt

⌐ Add minced fresh thyme and sage leaves to the rosemary salt for more flavor.

Bring the potato to a boil in a pot of cold salted water. When tender, drain, peel and mash.
Preheat the oven to 400°F (200°C or Gas Mark 6).
Prepare the focaccia dough following the recipe on page 384. Add the mashed potato to the dough and finish kneading. Roll out the dough into a sheet about about ⅛-inch (3 mm) thick. Cut out as many 3-inch (8 cm) rounds as possible. Place the rounds on an oiled baking sheet and let rise for 20 minutes.
Brush with olive oil and bake for 10-15 minutes. Meanwhile, mix the rosemary with the coarse salt. Remove the focaccias from the oven and slice them in half while still hot.
Place a slice of lardo between the 2 halves and season with a pinch of the rosemary salt. Serve immediately.

Preparation time **15 minutes**
Cooking time **15 minutes**
Level **easy**
Wine **Prosecco di Conegliano e Valdobbiadene Brut**

calabrian mozzarella parcels

Ingredients for 4 servings

Dough:

1¾ tsps (12 g) active dry yeast

7 tbsps water

salt

1 tbsp extra-virgin olive oil

1½ cups plus 1½ tbsps (7 oz or 200 g) all-purpose flour

Filling:

3½ oz (100 g) sun-dried San Marzano tomatoes

1 tbsp salted capers

5 oz (150 g) mozzarella cheese, diced

oregano

sunflower oil

Prepare the dough following the recipe for panzerotti on page 387.
Cover the sun-dried tomatoes with lukewarm water and leave to soak for an hour. Drain and dry, then roughly chop. Rinse the capers, changing the water at least 3 times. Drain and chop. Mix the tomatoes, mozzarella and capers in a bowl with the oregano.
Roll out the dough on a floured work surface. Cut into small squares. Place a spoonful of filling in the center of each square, and then fold in the edges, pressing gently to seal the dough together. Heat the sunflower oil then fry the parcels until golden. Drain and dry on paper towels. Sprinkle with salt and serve immediately.

⌐ Try using sun-dried tomatoes that have been rehydrated and marinated in olive oil.

Preparation time **15 minutes**
Cooking time **5 minutes**
Level **easy**
Wine **Cirò Bianco**

panzerotti with prosciutto and gruyère

Ingredients for 4-6 servings

3½ oz (100 g) Gruyère cheese, diced

3½ oz (100 g) prosciutto, diced

1 egg

2 tbsps grated Parmesan cheese

salt and pepper

3/4 cup plus 1 tbsp (3½ oz or 100 g) all-purpose flour

4 tbsps (2 oz or 50 g) room-temperature butter, diced

2 egg yolks

1/2 cup (3½ oz or 100 g) lard

Mix together the Gruyère, prosciutto and egg and season with pinches of salt and pepper.
Mound the flour on a work surface and make a well in the center. Add a pinch of salt, the butter, egg yolks and enough water to form a smooth dough.
Roll out the dough into a sheet of medium thickness. Cut out as many rounds as possible using a cookie cutter. Place a spoonful of filling in the center and fold into half-moon shapes.
Seal by pressing down on the edges with a fork.
Melt the lard in a large frying pan and when hot, fry the panzerotti until golden-brown on both sides.
Drain using a slotted spoon and place on paper towels.
Serve very hot.

If the edges of the panzerotti will not close tightly, brush them with a little beaten egg white before pressing them shut with a fork.

Preparation time **40 minutes**
Cooking time **20 minutes**
Level **medium**
Wine **Bianco dei Colli Albani**

mushroom and goat's cheese rolls

Ingredients for 4 servings

Crêpes:

3/4 cup plus 1 tbsp (3½ oz or 100 g) all-purpose flour

1 egg

1 cup (250 ml) milk, salt

Filling:

2 small fresh porcini mushrooms

5½ oz (150 g) soft goat's milk cheese

2 tbsps extra-virgin olive oil

fresh mint leaves, minced

salt and pepper

1 head of frisée lettuce, shredded

Mix together the flour, egg, milk and a pinch of salt in a food processor. Let rest for 20 minutes.
Meanwhile, clean the mushrooms with a damp paper towel, cut away any rough or muddy areas and thinly slice them. Strain the batter through a wire mesh sieve.
Heat a non-stick pan over medium heat and pour in a ladleful of batter. Turn the pan to make an even layer.
Flip the crêpe and cook until it begins to color.
Make 3 more large crêpes and let them cool for 5 minutes.
Beat the goat's cheese with a fork, add the olive oil and mint and season to taste with salt and pepper.
Spread the cheese filling over the crepes and top with the mushrooms and the lettuce.
Roll up the crêpes and slice into smaller lengths before serving.

For another vegetarian appetizer spread the crêpes with green olive tapenade, sprinkle over a handful of pine nuts and top with julienned carrots. Roll up and slice before serving.

Preparation time **25 minutes**
Cooking time **10 minutes**
Level **easy**
Wine **Alto Adige Gewürztraminer**

panzerotti with provola and sausage

Ingredients for 4 servings

1½ tsps active dry yeast

7 tbsps water

1 tbsp extra-virgin olive oil

salt and pepper

1⅔ cups (7 oz or 200 g) all-purpose flour

7 oz (200 g) sausage

5½ oz (150 g) mild provola or provolone cheese, diced

1 egg, beaten

sunflower oil

Prepare the panzerotti dough following the recipe on page 387. Remove the casing from the sausage and crumble up the meat. Mix the sausage with the cheese and sprinkle with a small pinch of pepper. Stir the mixture to combine. Flour a work surface and roll out small quantities of dough into thick but small rounds.
Trim the rounds into regular shapes and fill them with the sausage mixture. Fold in half, brush the edges with the beaten egg and pinch closed.
Heat the sunflower oil in a small pot.
Fry the panzerotti in small batches until golden-brown on both sides. Drain with a slotted spoon, sprinkle with salt and serve immediately.

For a stronger flavored filling, try using spicy or smoked provola or provolone in place of the mild provola cheese.

Preparation time **10 minutes**
Cooking time **5 minutes**
Level **easy**
Wine **Lambrusco di Sorbara**

sautéed artichoke and chicken liver crostini

Ingredients for 4 servings

1 lb (500 g) tender baby artichokes
3 tbsps extra-virgin olive oil
parsley
1 garlic clove, smashed
salt
10½ oz (300 g) chicken livers, finely chopped
1 tab of butter
10 sage leaves, minced
1/4 cup (60 ml) dry white wine
4 slices crusty Tuscan-style bread

Remove the tough outer leaves from the artichokes, halve them and remove the heart.
Heat the olive oil in a frying pan and add the artichokes, a few sprigs of parsley, the garlic clove and a few tablespoons of water. Let cook over medium heat until tender. Season to taste with salt.
Meanwhile, sauté the chicken livers in a pan with the butter and sage. Pour over the white wine and let cook off. Toast the bread slices in the toaster or under the grill. Top the bread slices with the chicken livers and artichokes and serve immediately.

Preparation time **20 minutes**
Cooking time **20 minutes**
Level **medium**
Wine **Bardolino Chiaretto**

tomato and tuma ravioli

Ingredients for 4 servings

4 cups (1 lb 1½ oz or 500 g) all-purpose flour

salt and pepper

3 small tomatoes, blanched, peeled and sliced

6 anchovies packed in salt, rinsed

1 bunch of parsley, minced

9 oz (250 g) tuma cheese (see note), diced

sunflower oil

Mound the flour on a work surface and make a well in the center. Add a pinch of salt and enough water to form a smooth dough. Let rest for 1 hour. Meanwhile, place the tomatoes in a bowl and crumble in the anchovy fillets. Add the parsley and cheese and season to taste with salt and pepper. Mix well. Roll out the dough into a thin sheet cut out rounds with a cookie cutter.
Place a spoonful of filling in the center and fold in half, making a half-moon shape. Pinch the edges closed. Heat the sunflower oil in a saucepan and fry the ravioli in small batches. When the ravioli begin to brown, remove with a slotted spoon and place on paper towels to dry. Serve immediately.

Tuma is an aged goat's milk cheese of Sardinian origin. If it is unavailable, use a fresh sheep's milk cheese.

Preparation time **20 minutes**
Cooking time **15 minutes**
Level **easy**
Wine **Torbato di Alghero**

piadinas with swiss chard and scamorza

Ingredients for 4 servings

Dough:
- 4 cups (1 lb 1½ oz or 500 g) all-purpose flour
- 3 tbsps lard
- salt
- 1 garlic clove, halved

Filling:
- 8 cups (10½ oz or 300 g) chopped Swiss chard
- salt and pepper
- 2 tbsps extra-virgin olive oil
- 3½ oz (100 g) scamorza, sliced

Prepare the piadinas following the recipe on page 387. Rub the piadinas with the garlic clove.
Blanch the chard in boiling salted water until tender. Season with salt and pepper. Place the chard on top of 2 piadinas. Drizzle with olive oil and top with the scamorza. Top with the remaining piadinas to form a sandwich and cook in a hot non-stick pan until the cheese melts, about 3 minutes.
Cut the piadinas in half and serve immediately.

For a delicious variation, use grilled eggplant and sliced mozzarella for the filling.

Preparation time **10 minutes**
Cooking time **15 minutes**
Level **easy**
Wine **Trebbiano di Romagna**

fried pumpkin tortelli

Ingredients for 4 servings

7 oz (200 g) lardo (cured lard), chopped

2 garlic cloves

2 lb (1 kg) pumpkin, peeled, seeded and sliced

2 eggs

salt and pepper

8 cups (2 lb or 1 kg) all-purpose flour

sunflower oil

Preheat the oven to 375°F (190°C or Gas Mark 5). Render the lardo in a frying pan with the garlic cloves. Bake the pumpkin for 40 minutes, until tender. Remove from the oven, cool and cut into small pieces.
Mix in the eggs and toss together with the lardo and garlic cloves. Season to taste with salt and pepper and mix well. Mix together the flour and salt with enough water to form a smooth dough of medium consistency.
Roll out the dough on a lightly floured work surface and cut it into 4-inch (10 cm) squares.
Place a spoonful of filling on each square and fold in half to form the tortelli. Pinch the edges to seal and fry in hot sunflower oil until golden brown. Drain on paper towels, season with a pinch of salt and serve hot.

⌐ A wooden board called a *spianatoia* is frequently used for making pasta and pastry doughs in Italy. The board must be perfectly flat and should be stored in a dry place with a constant temperature so that it won't bend out of shape.

Preparation time **40 minutes**
Cooking time **45 minutes**
Level **medium**
Wine **Trebbiano di Romagna Spumante**

chicken tacos with guacamole

Ingredients for 4 servings

Tacos:

2 tbsps extra-virgin olive oil
1 medium onion, minced
1 hot red chili pepper, deseeded and diced
1 garlic clove, smashed
7 oz (200 g) chicken meat, diced or ground
8 tortillas, 1 tomato, diced
8 tbsps hot sauce or salsa

Guacamole:

1 ripe avocado, peeled and pitted
1 cilantro sprig, chopped
1 tbsp lemon juice, ¼ onion, chopped

Garnish:

1 red tomato, diced
1/2 onion, thinly sliced
lettuce, shredded, hot sauce

Heat the olive oil in a frying pan and sauté the onion, chili and garlic for the tacos until soft.
Add the chicken and sauté until cooked through.
Fill the tortillas with the chicken mixture, tomato and hot sauce or salsa. Roll them up or fold them in half.
Heat a non-stick frying pan and sear the tacos for 2 minutes.
To make the guacamole, mix the avocado, cilantro, lemon juice and onion in a food processor or mash with a fork.
Serve the tacos with the guacamole, diced tomato, onion rings, lettuce and hot sauce.

Preparation time **15 minutes**
Cooking time **5 minutes**
Level **easy**
Wine **Enfer d'Arvier**

spiced beef triangles

Ingredients for 4 servings

2 lb (1 kg) ground beef

3 large onions, thinly sliced

4 garlic cloves, minced

1 inch (2½-cm) piece of fresh ginger, minced

1 tbsp curry

1 tbsp turmeric

2 lb (1 kg) prepared pizza dough all-purpose flour

1 egg, beaten

sunflower oil, salt

Mix together the ground beef, onions, garlic, ginger, curry and turmeric.
Brown the beef in a frying pan over low heat for about 30 minutes, stirring from time to time. Pour off the fat. Roll out the dough on a lightly floured work surface and cut it into 4-inch (10 cm) long strips.
Fold the rectangles in half to form a triangle, fill the pocket that is formed with the meat filling and fold the edge over. Brush the edges with beaten egg and pinch to seal. Heat abundant sunflower oil and fry the triangles until golden. Drain, season with salt and serve immediately.

beyond sandwiches

Turmeric is weed from the Middle East. The root of the plant is treated and ground to make the bright yellow-colored spice. Turmeric is one of the many spices commonly used in curry mixtures.

Preparation time **20 minutes**
Cooking time **25 minutes**
Level **easy**
Wine **Sicilia Cabernet-Sauvignon**

chickpea crêpes with winter squash

Ingredients for 4 servings

Crêpes:

2 eggs, salt

2 cups (500 ml) milk

1 tbsp extra-virgin olive oil

1 cup (½ oz or 125 g) all-purpose flour

3/4 cup (2½ oz or 70 g) chickpea flour

1 tsp poppy seeds

Filling:

1/2 green-skinned winter squash (such as Kabocha), peeled, deseeded and thinly sliced

1 tbsp extra-virgin olive oil

4 tbsps heavy cream

salt and pepper, sunflower oil

Preheat the oven to 375°F (190°C or Gas Mark 5). Mix together the eggs, salt, milk and olive oil and gradually sift in the different flours. Let the batter rest for 20 minutes, then pass it through a sieve to remove any lumps. Stir in the poppy seeds. Place the squash on a baking sheet, reserving a small slice for garnish. Brush with olive oil and bake for 25 minutes. Remove from the oven, cool slightly and puree the squash together with the cream.
Season to taste with salt and pepper.
Make the crêpes in a lightly oiled non-stick frying pan. Fill each one with a little squash puree, fold in half and then in half again to make a triangle. Julienne the reserved squash and fry it in abundant sunflower oil.
Top the crêpes with the fried squash and serve.

For added flavor, add a grating of fresh nutmeg to the squash filling.

Preparation time **10 minutes**
Cooking time **30 minutes**
Level **easy**
Wine **Valcalepio Bianco**

flatbreads with lardo and rosemary

Ingredients for 4 servings

2⅓ cups plus 1 tbsp (10½ oz or 300 g) all-purpose flour

salt

2 oz (50 g) lardo (cured lard), minced

1 garlic clove, minced

rosemary, minced

1 piece of pork rind

9 tbsps grated Parmesan cheese

Mix together the flour and salt and add enough water for form a batter of medium consistency. Set aside. Using a mortar and pestle, combine the lardo, garlic and rosemary.
Heat a frying pan and grease it with the pork rind. When very hot, pour in a ladleful of batter and turn the pan to make an even layer. Let cook for a few seconds, fill and cook for another few seconds.
Remove from the pan and spread the rosemary mixture over the flatbread. Sprinkle with Parmesan.
Continue making the flatbreads until all of the batter has been used up. Serve the flatbreads hot.

⌐ The lardo may be replaced by a puree of 3½ oz (100 g) prosciutto and 2½ oz (70 g) stracchino or other fresh, spreadable cheese.

Preparation time **20 minutes**
Cooking time **5 minutes**
Level **easy**
Wine **Colli Bolognesi Barbera**

baguette stuffed with ham mousse

Ingredients for 6-8 servings
12½ oz (350 g) ham, diced
11 tbsps (5½ oz or 150 g) softened butter
3½ oz (100 g) mixed vegetables preserved in vinegar
1 bunch of arugula, coarsely chopped
salt and pepper
2 baguettes

Puree the ham and the butter together until smooth. Drain the vegetables and coarsely chop them. Mix the arugula and vegetables into the ham mousse and season to taste with salt and pepper.
Cut the baguettes in half lengthwise and remove some of the crumb. Spread a thick layer of mousse over the bread, close and wrap in plastic wrap. Refrigerate until cold and slice on the diagonal into 3-inch (7 cm) lengths.

Baguettes were supposedly invented during the Industrial Revolution. In Paris in the early 19th century the law dictating the working hours for bakers was changed and they could no longer start work before 4 am. The baguette was the only type of bread that bakers could prepare in time for their early-morning customers.

Preparation time **20 minutes**
Level **easy**
Wine **Lambrusco di Sorbara**

fennel and finocchiona crostini

Ingredients for 4 servings

1 fennel bulb, very thinly sliced

salt and pepper

3 tbsps extra-virgin olive oil

1 bunch of wild fennel or dill, minced

1 loaf of crusty bread

1⅓ lb (600 g) finocchiona or other salami, very thinly sliced

Place the fennel in a mixing bowl and season it with a pinch of salt and freshly ground pepper.
Drizzle over the olive oil and add the wild fennel.
Toss to coat and let sit as long as possible.
Cut the bread into ½-inch (1 cm) thick slices and toast it under the grill for 5 minutes.
Place a spoonful of the fennel on each slice of toasted bread and top with 2 slices of finocchiona.
Garnish with fennel and serve immediately.

A mandolin is used to slice vegetables in various shapes, sizes and thicknesses. It is named after the instrument because the movement made when slicing with a mandolin is similar to the one used when playing the musical instrument.

Preparation time **15 minutes**
Cooking time **5 minutes**
Level **easy**
Wine **Rosso di Montalcino**

ham, cheese and fried egg sandwiches

Ingredients for 4 servings

3 tbsps mustard
8 slices of fresh bread
4 eggs
1 tbsp extra-virgin olive oil
4 tbsps (2 oz or 50 g) butter
10½ oz (300 g) smoked ham, thinly sliced
5½ oz (150 g) melting cheese (mild fontina or Camembert), sliced

Spread the mustard on the bread.
Fry the eggs in an oiled non-stick pan.
Top 4 slices of bread with a slice of ham, 1 fried egg and 1 slice of cheese. Cover with the remaining bread slices. Butter the outside of sandwiches and brown them on both sides in a hot frying pan. Serve hot.

The smoked ham may be substituted with cooked bacon and the fontina with the same quantity of thinly sliced Brie.

Preparation time **15 minutes**
Cooking time **10 minutes**
Level **easy**
Wine **Prosecco di Conegliano e Valdobbiadene Brut**

piadinas with prosciutto, buffalo mozzarella, grilled tomatoes and basil

Ingredients for 4 servings
Dough:
4 cups (1 lb 1½ oz or 500 g) all-purpose flour
3 tbsps lard, water, salt
Filling:
3 tomatoes, thickly sliced
1 pinch of oregano, salt
11 oz (300 g) buffalo's milk mozzarella, thinly sliced
3½ oz (100 g) prosciutto, thinly sliced
2 tbsps extra-virgin olive oil
1 bunch of basil

Prepare the piadinas following the recipe on page 387. Heat a ridged cast-iron pan and grill the tomato slices for 1 minute on each side. Sprinkle with salt and oregano. Fill the warm piadinas with mozzarella, prosciutto and tomato. Season with salt and olive oil and add basil leaves. Fold over and serve immediately.

The warm tomatoes and cold mozzarella give this dish a pleasant contrast.

Preparation time **15 minutes**
Cooking time **5 minutes**
Level **easy**
Wine **Tocai Friulano**

buckwheat tortelli with ricotta and spinach

Ingredients for 6 servings
1 2/3 cups (200 g) buckwheat flour
1 2/3 cups (200 g) all-purpose flour
salt
1 tbsp extra-virgin olive oil
milk
6 2/3 cups (7 oz or 200 g) spinach
7 oz (200 g) ricotta
sunflower oil

Mound the different flours on a work surface. Make a well in the center and add a pinch of salt, the olive oil and enough milk to form a smooth dough. Roll into a ball and let rest for 30 minutes.
Roll the dough into a thick log and slice into rounds. Roll out the rounds with a rolling pin. Blanch the spinach in salted water.
Drain and finely chop. Mix the ricotta and spinach together and season to taste with salt.
Place a spoonful of filling on half of the rounds.
Top with the remaining dough rounds and seal the edges, pressing down with a fork. Heat abundant sunflower oil in a saucepan and fry the tortelli until golden-brown on both sides. Drain with a slotted spoon and serve hot.

The spinach in the filling may be substituted with 7 oz (200 g) of cooked cabbage.

Preparation time **40 minutes**
Cooking time **30 minutes**
Level **easy**
Wine **Sorni Rosso**

meatball sandwiches with olive spread

Ingredients for 4 servings

7 oz (200 g) ground beef

1 cup (3½ oz or 100 g) grated Parmesan cheese

1⅓ cups (5½ oz or 150 g) breadcrumbs

1 egg, salt and pepper

4 tbsps extra-virgin olive oil

2 oz (50 g) pitted green olives, chopped

5½ oz (150 g) soft, spreadable cheese

3 tomatoes

4 mini baguettes, halved lengthwise

4 tbsps bell pepper spread

4 lettuce leaves

Mix together the ground beef, Parmesan, breadcrumbs and the egg. Season with pinches of salt and pepper. Roll the mixture into balls and press them into ovals. Fry in the olive oil for 10 minutes.
Mix the olives and the cheese until smooth and spreadable. Slice the tomatoes and lightly salt them. Spread one half of the each roll with bell pepper spread and top with 1 lettuce leaf, a meatball, a few slices of tomato and the olive spread.
Place the tops on the sandwiches and serve immediately.

Potato bread or any other soft roll may be used in place of the French bread rolls in this recipe.

Preparation time **10 minutes**
Cooking time **10 minutes**
Level **easy**
Wine **Gutturnio Classico**

mini focaccia panini with grilled vegetables

Ingredients for 4 servings

1 eggplant, sliced
salt and pepper
extra-virgin olive oil
2 tomatoes, sliced
oregano
9 oz (250 g) focaccia bread
2 whole fresh mozzarellas
3 eggs, hard-boiled, peeled and sliced

Salt the eggplant slices and place the in a colander with a weighted plate on top. Let sit for 30 minutes.
Dry and grill the eggplant slices in a ridged cast-iron grill pan. Transfer to a plate and season to taste with salt and pepper and drizzle with olive oil.
Season the tomato slices with salt, pepper and oregano and drizzle with olive oil.
Slice the focaccia in half. Layer over the mozzarella slices, grilled eggplant, tomato and egg. Season with oregano and cover with the top of the focaccia. Cut into small squares and secure with toothpicks.

The egg may be replaced with 7 oz (200 g) of finely chopped black olives.

Preparation time **10 minutes**
Cooking time **7 minutes**
Level **easy**
Wine **Greco di Tufo**

bruschetta with zucchini, carrots and peppers

Ingredients for 4 servings

4 tbsps extra-virgin olive oil
1 shallot, finely minced
1/2 red bell pepper, deseeded and diced
2 carrots, thinly sliced
2 zucchini
salt and pepper
10 black olives, pitted and halved
1 loaf of whole-wheat bread, sliced

Preheat the oven to 350°F (180°C or Gas Mark 4). Heat 2 tablespoons of olive oil in a frying pan and sauté the shallot until soft. Add the diced pepper and sauté for a few minutes. Add the carrots and continue cooking. Trim the zucchini, quarter them lengthwise, remove the white seedy part and dice the rest.
Add to the other vegetables. Season with salt and pepper and continue cooking until all the vegetables are soft. Stir in the olives. Drizzle the bread slices with olive oil and toast in the oven for 5 minutes.
Remove from the oven and serve topped with the sautéed vegetables.

To make the topping even more flavorful, roast the bell pepper over an open flame or under a broiler until blackened, then close in a plastic bag to steam. When cool, peel, deseed and dice, then add to the already-cooked zucchini and carrots.

Preparation time **20 minutes**
Cooking time **20 minutes**
Level **easy**
Wine **Malvasia Istriana**

truffled leek panzerotti

Ingredients for 4 servings

1 cup (5½ oz or 150 g) all-purpose flour

3 tbsps extra-virgin olive oil, salt

3 tbsps water

1 tsp lard

1 tab of butter

1 leek, thinly sliced

3½ oz (100 g) whole-wheat bread, sliced

3/4 cup (200 ml) milk

1 tbsp truffle oil

1 white truffle, ½ minced and ½ shaved

sunflower oil

Place the flour in a bowl and add the olive oil, salt, water and lard. Mix vigorously then transfer to a floured work surface and continue kneading until a smooth and elastic dough is obtained. Form into a ball, wrap in plastic wrap and refrigerate. Melt the butter in a saucepan and sauté the leek with a little water until transparent.
Soak the bread in the milk until soft, then squeeze out excess milk. Add to the leeks together with truffle oil. Let cool, then stir in the minced truffle.
Roll out the dough and form large round ravioli stuffed with the leek mixture. Seal the edges well.
Heat the sunflower oil until very hot and fry the panzerotti. Serve hot garnished with the remaining shaved truffle.

White truffles are the most expensive and prized of the different kinds of truffles. They are highly fragrant and available only for a short period of the year. The best are from around Alba, in Piedmont.

Preparation time **25 minutes**
Cooking time **15 minutes**
Level **easy**
Wine **Dolcetto d'Alba**

beef and bean tacos

Ingredients for 4 servings

10½ oz (300 g) beef sirloin

salt

2 tbsps sunflower oil

8 corn tortillas

1 medium onion, finely chopped

2 tomatoes, diced

1/2 cup (125 g) refried beans

8 lettuce leaves, shredded

1/2 cup (120 ml) sour cream

3½ oz (100 g) mild white cheese

Sear the in the beef in a very hot non-stick pan until medium rare, turning so that the meat browns evenly on all sides. Remove from the pan and let cool.
Dice and lightly salt. Meanwhile, heat the sunflower oil in a frying pan and sauté the onions.
Add the tomatoes and the beef sauté briefly and remove from heat. Heat the tortillas in a non-stick pan or fry them briefly in 2 tablespoons on sunflower oil.
Remove from heat and place on work surface.
Spread the refried beans over the fried tortillas and top with the lettuce. Add the sautéed meat mixture and grated cheese and drizzle with sour cream.
Fold the tortillas in half before serving.

Tacos are a traditional Mexican dish. For a rich and tasty variation, top the tacos with freshly made guacamole.

Preparation time **30 minutes**
Cooking time **45 minutes**
Level **easy**
Wine **Malbec Argentino**

parma-style fritters

Ingredients for 4-6 servings

4 cups (1 lb 1½ oz or 500 g) all-purpose flour

3 tbsps extra-virgin olive oil

salt

lard

Mound the flour on a work surface and make a well at the center. Add the olive oil, salt and enough water to form a smooth, soft dough.
Roll out the dough out very thinly and cut it into diamond shapes. Melt the lard in a frying pan over high heat. When it begins to boil, fry the pieces of dough until golden brown on both sides.
Drain and let dry on paper towels. Serve hot.

Serve this dish as an appetizer accompanied by a selection of thinly sliced salami and other cured meats.

Preparation time **15 minutes**
Cooking time **5 minutes**
Level **easy**
Wine **Colli di Parma Rosso**

polenta bread with sausage

Ingredients for 8-10 servings

1/3 cup plus 2 tbsps (2 oz or 60 g) raisins

2 lbs (1 kg) cornmeal for polenta

9 oz (250 g) sausage

4 tbsps extra-virgin olive oil

salt and pepper

Soak the raisins in a little warm water for at least 10 minutes. Pour the cornmeal into a large bowl and add enough water to form a very thick batter.
Crumble the sausage into a frying pan and brown with a little olive oil until cooked through. Let cool slightly and add to the batter. Drain the raisins, squeeze out the excess liquid and add to the batter. Season with pinches of salt and pepper. Oil a round cake pan and pour in the batter. Smooth the top and drizzle with olive oil.
Bake until the top is golden-brown (30 minutes).
Slice and serve hot.

Raisins are dried grapes, and the different types depend on the type of grape used. Sultanas are golden in color, sweet and juicy, and are among the best for cooking purposes.

Preparation time **15 minutes**
Cooking time **30 minutes**
Level **easy**
Wine **Lagrein Rosato**

crispy rosemary flatbread

Ingredients for 4 servings

1¼ cups (5½ oz or 150 g) all-purpose flour

4 tbsps sunflower oil

2 tbsps extra-virgin olive oil

2 rosemary sprigs, coarsely chopped

sea salt flakes

Preheat the oven to 485°F (250°C or Gas Mark 8).
Pour the flour into a mixing bowl and add the sunflower oil, olive oil and a little water. Add half of the rosemary and mix with the fingertips to combine.
Transfer the dough to a work surface and knead vigorously. Add more flour or water if the dough seems too wet or dry. Continue to work the dough until it is smooth and elastic. Roll into a ball and wrap in plastic wrap. Refrigerate for about 20 minutes.
Divide the dough into small portions and roll out each one into a very thin sheet with a pasta machine.
Place the dough sheets on a baking sheet and sprinkle with the remaining rosemary and sea salt.
Bake for 4 minutes, remove from the oven and cool before serving.

Serve the flatbread with a spicy salsa or a creamy cheese.

Preparation time **10 minutes**
Cooking time **4 minutes**
Level **easy**
Wine **Elba Bianco**

chapati

Ingredients for 4 servings

3½ cups (1 lb 1½ oz or 500 g) whole-wheat flour

salt

peanut oil

1/2 tsp butter

Mix almost all the flour (reserve 4 tablespoons) with a pinch of salt, a drizzle of peanut oil, the butter and a few tablespoons of water. Continue mixing and add up to 2 cups (500 ml) of water. The dough should have the consistency of pizza dough. Knead the dough until smooth and elastic. Divide the dough into balls about the size of a tennis ball and let rest for 10 minutes. Dust each ball of dough with flour and flatten it out with the hands. Roll out the dough into a thin, even round about 1/5-inch (3 mm) thick.
Heat a non-stick pan on the stove.
Place 1 sheet of dough in the pan, making sure that it has no wrinkles or overlaps. When the dough begins to puff up and brown flip it and cook the other side for another minute or so.

Chapatis are a typical Indian flatbread made from finely ground whole-wheat flour. The breads have many names in India, including atta or hatta. Chapati bread can accompany stewed meats or vegetables in sauce.

Preparation time **15 minutes**
Cooking time **10 minutes**
Level **easy**
Wine **Prosecco di Valdobbiadene Brut**

cecina

Ingredients for 8 servings

6 cups (1½ l) water

3 cups (10½ oz or 300 g) chickpea flour

6 tbsps extra-virgin olive oil

salt and pepper

Preheat the oven to 425°F (220°C or Gas Mark 7).
Pour the water into a large mixing bowl. Sprinkle in the chickpea flour little by little, whisking constantly so that lumps do not form.
Drizzle in the olive oil and 1 teaspoon of salt. Mix to obtain a smooth batter and let rest for 30 minutes.
Oil a round, low-rimmed baking sheet and pour in the batter. Bake until a golden-brown crust forms on the top, about 30 minutes. Remove from the oven and season with freshly ground pepper. Serve hot.

Cecina is a very wide and thin savory tart, almost like a crêpe, bright yellow from the chickpea flour. It has a soft interior and a crunchy exterior. It is an ancient recipe that has changed little over the years. It should be eaten seasoned with freshly ground pepper.

Preparation time **5 minutes**
Cooking time **30 minutes**
Level **easy**
Wine **Bianco Vergine della Valdichiana**

piadina romagnola

Ingredients for 4-6 servings
8 cups (2 lbs or 1 kg) all-purpose flour
3/4 cup (5½ oz or 150 g) lard
salt
milk or water

Mound the flour on a work surface and make a well in the center. Place the lard and a pinch of salt in the well and work with fingertips to form a ropy dough.
Add enough milk or water to form a smooth and elastic dough and knead well.
Roll into a ball, cover with a kitchen towel and let rest for about 1 hour.
Divide the dough into many small balls and roll each one into a thin round, about 10 inches (25 cm) in diameter.
Cook the piadinas in a very hot cast-iron pan or on a griddle. Spin the piadinas in a clockwise direction as they cook, and pierce them with the tines of a fork.
Flip and cook the other side.
Serve the piadinas hot, filled, if desired, with cheese or cured meats.

The piadina is a classic unleavened bread from Romagna. It is often served with pancetta, sausage or squacquerone cheese and arugula. The variations for fillings are numerous and depend only on the creativity of the cook. In the past this bread was cooked on a stone griddle heated over coals.

Preparation time **30 minutes**
Cooking time **10 minutes**
Level **easy**
Wine **Trebbiano di Romagna Spumante**

basic techniques

Pizza

BASIC DOUGH RECIPES

In the following chapter, readers will find basic recipes for pizza, focaccia and savory tart crusts.

Pizza Dough

Ingredients for 1½ lb (700 g) pizza dough
2 tsps (16 g) active dry yeast; **1** cup (250 ml) warm water; **2** tsps salt; **1** tsp sugar; **4** tbsps extra-virgin olive oil; **4** cups (1 lb 1½ oz or 500 g) all-purpose flour

Dissolve the yeast in the warm water. Add the salt, sugar and olive oil and whisk together. Sift the flour onto a work surface and make a well at the center. Pour the yeast mixture into the well and mix with the fingertips until the liquid has been incorporated. Knead vigorously to form a smooth and elastic dough. Cover with a kitchen towel and let rise for 2 hours. Punch down the dough and then divide it into small portions. Cover and let rise for another hour.

Variations

When making pizza dough, reinforced or bread flour may replace some of the all-purpose flour. This type of flour is higher in protein and requires a longer rising time. Alternatively special pizza flour, a blend of bread flour and all-purpose flour, is available at supermarkets and specialty stores.
For a crunchier crust, add an egg yolk to the dough. Not only will this give the pizza a crispy texture it will give the pizza crust a golden color.
Be careful when salting the dough as too much salt will stop the yeast from fermenting and the dough will not rise correctly. To facilitate fermentation, add a tablespoon of malt powder or a little sugar to the dough.
Whole-wheat pizza makes a nutritious alternative: Mix 4 cups (1 lb 1½ oz 500 g) whole-wheat flour with 2 tablespoons extra-virgin olive oil, 3¼ teaspoons (25 g) active dry yeast and enough water to form a smooth dough. Knead for about 10 minutes, cover and let rise for 1 hour 30 minutes.

Curiosity
Try adding boiled mashed potatoes (5½ oz or 150 g potatoes for every 4 cups 1 lb or 500 g of flour) to the pizza dough.
The addition of potatoes makes a perfect dough for pizzas and focaccias that are pan-fried.

Baking

While baking the pizza may seem simple, it is important to remember a few basic techniques that help make the perfect crust. The best way to cook pizza is in a traditional wood-fired oven, and authentic pizza restaurants still prefer a wood-fired oven to the modern electric ovens. Both wood-fired and industrial ovens reach higher temperatures, from 575° to 660°F (300° to 350°C), and allow a shorter cooking time for the pizza. Conventional home ovens cannot reach such high temperatures and consequently home-made pizzas require longer cooking times, about 20 minutes. Cooking a pizza for too long can have a negative effect on the rising dough.

Thicker crust pizzas are a better choice when making pizza at home, and many home cooks add a pan of hot water to create moisture in the oven, so that the crust will not dry out. Remember to spread the sauce on the pizza immediately after placing it in the baking sheet and to add the mozzarella halfway though the baking so it doesn't burn.

Pizza Napoletana

In 2004 the Neapolitan-style pizza was classified as a "Guaranteed Traditional Specialty" or STG. In order to maintain the classification the pizza must be prepared using specific ingredients and following traditional methods. About 4 lb (1.8 kg) of flour are used for every 4 cups (1 liter) of water, 2 oz (50 g) of salt and 2/3 tsp (5 g) of fresh yeast.

The flour must be added slowly to the water and kneaded for at least 20 minutes or until the dough is puffy and smooth to the touch. Its consistency should be stretchy but not too elastic.

The dough is left to rise on a marble surface, covered with a damp towel to prevent a dry crust from forming over the surface, for 4 hours. The dough is then divided into balls weighing about 7 oz (200 g) each. The dough is never rolled with a rolling pin but pushed and tossed with the hands.

Tip
Buffalo mozzarella adds flavor and richness to any pizza. It is preserved in liquid and has a high moisture content so it is important to drain the cheese and let it dry out a little before adding it to the pizza, otherwise it can make the pizza soggy.

The classic pizza napoletana is topped with San Marzano tomato sauce, buffalo mozzarella from Campania and olive oil. It is baked in a wood-fired oven with a refractory tile hearth and dome-shaped interior made from refractory bricks at a temperature that can vary from 825° - 900°F (450° - 485°C). The pizza is turned frequently to allow for even cooking and is baked for a very short amount of time. A true pizza napoletana can be made at home only using a wood-fired oven.

Focaccia

Ingredients for 1½ lb (700 g) focaccia dough
3¼ tsps (25 g) active dry yeast; **4** cups (1 lb 1½ oz 500 g) all-purpose flour; **4** tbsps (2 oz or 50 g) butter; **1** tsp salt; extra-virgin olive oil

Dissolve the yeast in a little water. Mound the flour on a work surface and make a well in the center. Pour in the yeast mixture, butter and salt and begin to mix using the fingertips. Add enough water to form a medium consistency dough. Knead until smooth and elastic. Coat the dough with olive oil and let rise, covered, for 15 minutes. Divide the dough into portions and form into balls. Let rise for another 10 minutes.
Preheat the oven to 480°F (250°C or Gas Mark 9).
Spread the dough onto an oiled baking sheet using the fingertips and drizzle with olive oil. Let rise for another 30 minutes, then bake until golden-brown. The cooking time will depend on the size and thickness of the focaccia.

Variations
The best-known type of focaccia is Ligurian, made with extra-virgin olive oil and "oiled" to perfection. It has characteristic dimples that serve to hold little pools of oil and salt. To make Ligurian-style focaccia: Dissolve 1¾ tsps active dry yeast in a little water and add it to a little flour to make a fluid dough or thick batter. Let the starter rise for 30 minutes.

Tip
Make a spicy chili-infused oil to keep on hand: infuse 8-10 whole red chili peppers in 4 cups (1 l) good quality extra-virgin olive oil. Let sit for 15-20 days before using. This oil is perfect for drizzling over pizzas and focaccias.

Mound 3½ cups (1 lb 1½ oz 500 g) bread flour on a work surface and make a well in the center. Add the starter, a generous drizzle of olive oil and pinches of sugar and salt to the well. Mix together with the hands and then knead until smooth, adding more flour or water if necessary. Transfer the dough to a bowl, make an X-shaped incision on the top and let rise, covered, for at least 2 hours. Preheat the oven to 400°F (200°C or Gas Mark 6).

Line a rimmed baking sheet with parchment paper and coat the paper with abundant olive oil. Stretch out the dough and push it over the baking sheet using the hands and fingertips. The dough should form a relatively thin layer. Push down with the fingertips to make a series of dimples over the surface of the focaccia. Whisk together an emulsion of equal parts olive oil and water and sprinkle it over the focaccia. Sprinkle generously with coarse salt and let rise for 20 minutes. Bake for 30-40 minutes.

The famous Recco focaccia can also be made from this dough. Simply divide the dough in half, stretch half out over the baking sheet, top with 1 lb (500 g) of stracchino or other soft fresh cheese and top with the remaining dough. Let rise for 30 minutes and bake for 30-40 minutes at 400°F (200°C or Gas Mark 6).

Puff pastry

Ingredients for 1 lb (500 g) puff pastry:
1⅔ cups (7 oz or 200 g) all-purpose flour; **7** tbsps water; salt; **1** cup plus 1 tbsp (9 oz or 250 g) margarine

Mound the flour on a work surface and place the water and a pinch of salt in the center. Mix well to form an elastic dough. Wrap in a clean kitchen towel and let rest for 20 minutes. Roll out the dough into a very thin rectangular sheet (1/5 inch or ½ cm). Thinly slice the margarine and place it in the center of the dough. Fold the sides over the margarine and then fold the remaining two sides in. Roll out the dough very lightly with a rolling pin and then wrap in

Tip
Coarsely chop a handful of black or green pitted olives with a few capers, 1 tablespoon of toasted pine nuts, and a handful of julienned basil leaves. Add 1 tablespoon of olive oil and spread over the pizza just before it is done. Bake for another few minutes and serve.

aluminum foil and refrigerate for 5 minutes. Begin the first "round" of rolling out the dough; place the dough on a floured work surface and roll out the dough in one direction until it makes a 1/2-inch (1 cm) thick rectangle. Fold the dough in thirds horizontally to obtain a brick.

Turn the dough 90 degrees. Start the second round of rolling out the dough; roll out the dough in the same direction, fold into thirds, wrap in aluminum foil and refrigerate for 30 minutes. Repeat this operation 2 more times, turning and folding the dough a total of 6 times. After the final round, refrigerate for 1 hour before using.

Pâté brisée

Ingredients for 14 oz (400 g) pâté brisée
9 tbsps (4½ oz or 125 g) cold butter or margarine; **2⅓** cups plus 1 tbsp (10½ oz or 300 g) all-purpose flour; salt; **3½** tbsps cold water

Work the cold butter into the flour with the salt using the fingertips. When the mixture resembles coarse meal, add the cold water, little by little, and quickly work it into a dough. Roll the dough into a ball, cover with plastic wrap and refrigerate for at least 30 minutes before using.

Piadina Dough

This is the version of focaccia from the central region of Romagna. This unleavened flatbread has medieval origins, and makes the perfect accompaniment for cured meats, salami and cheeses.

Ingredients
4 cups (1 lb 1½ oz 500 g) all-purpose flour; **3** tbsps lard; 1 cup (250 ml) warm water; salt

Alternative
For a lighter piadina, add 1 tablespoon of baking soda and a drizzle of olive oil to the dough. Additionally, the thinner the dough is rolled out, the lighter and crispier the piadina will be.

Mound the flour on a work surface and make a well in the center. Dissolve the lard in a cup of warm water and add a generous pinch of salt. Pour the mixture into the well and mix together with the fingertips, adding a little warm water if necessary. Knead the dough until smooth and elastic (it should be a little bit softer than an egg pasta dough). Roll into a ball and wrap in plastic wrap or cover with a kitchen towel.

Let rest at room temperature. Divide the dough into small portions and roll out each one into a very thin round. Cook the piadinas on a cast iron griddle or pan for about 3 minutes on each side.

Panzerotti

Naples boasts a rich culinary tradition and panzerotti are one of the city's typical foods. The name panzerotto (singular of panzerotti) was given because of the puffy shape that is formed when the dough is cooked resembles a full belly (pancia). The basic panzerotti dough is similar to pizza dough, although it varies regionally.

Ingredients
1¾ tsps (12 g) active dry yeast; **7** tbsps warm water; salt; **1** tbsp extra-virgin olive oil; 1⅔ cups (7 oz or 200 g) all-purpose flour

Dissolve the yeast in warm water. Add a pinch of salt and the olive oil. Mound the dough on a work surface and make a well in the center.
Stir the yeast mixture and pour it into the well. Mix the dough with the fingertips and then knead until smooth and elastic. Cover with a damp kitchen towel and let rest for 30 minutes.

Suggestion
For a flavorful variation, add minced fresh herbs or finely chopped hazelnuts or pistachios to the panzerotti dough.

basic tools

Pizza

1 Oil Dispenser The best way to finish a pizza is with a drizzle of fresh extra-virgin olive oil. Oil cruets come in many shapes, sizes and materials. Stainless-steel containers are elegant and preserve olive oil and infused oils. Oil containers with drip stoppers are useful as they protect tablecloths and napkins.

2 Decorative Pizza Cutter A rolling pizza cutter is indispensable when cutting pizzas, focaccias and savory tarts. Both simple and decorative versions are available.

3 Serving Spatula This practical utensil is essential for serving pizzas, focaccias and savory tarts.

4 Serrated Serving Spatula One side of this serving spatula has a serrated blade that can slice through cakes, tarts or tortes.

5 Tomato Slicer The taut wires on this tool will cut a tomato into regular slices. It can also be used to cut mozzarella.

6 Large Rolling Pizza Cutter The large wheel on this pizza cutter will cut through the thickest of pizzas or focaccias without ruining the surface. This type of pizza cutter should have a safety guard to protect fingers.

7 Pizza Plate When entertaining, pizza plates can give a casual meal a refined touch. Larger than a regular plate, pizza plates will hold a whole pizza.

8 Cutting Board and Knife A large, decorative wooden cutting board is a practical way to serve whole pizzas at the table. It may also be used to present cured meats and cheeses.

9 Salt Mill The tastiest focaccia has dimples filled with olive oil and little flakes of salt. The salt should be ground to just the right size granule, not to fine or too large. Use a mill to freshly salt pizzas and focaccias at the last minute.

10 Expandable Baking Dish This innovative baking dish has a non-stick coating and it can be enlarged from 13 inches (33 cm) to 20 inches (52 cm).

11 Graters Graters with different-sized holes are necessary for grating cheese and other ingredients to the desired size. Silicon around the feet helps to hold the grater in place during use.

index

Pizza

Pizza

a
artichoke focaccia, 184
arugula and fresh cheese pizza, 124
asparagus bread, 266
asparagus fritters, 312
autumn pizza, 108

b
baby octopus, olive and caper pizza, 88
baguette stuffed with ham mousse, 348
baked ravioli, 302
beef and bean tacos, 366
bell pepper and smoked scamorza pizza, 112
bologna-style calzone, 44
broccoli and anchovy pizza, 86
bruschetta with zucchini, carrots and peppers, 362
buckwheat tortelli with ricotta and spinaci, 356
buffalo mozzarella pizza with green olive tapenade, 122

c
calabrian mozzarella parcels, 324
calabrian pizza with capers and eggplant, 106
calabrian-style pizza with 'ndjua, 56
capricciosa pizza, 24
carbonara pizza, 94
cardoon and salt cod strudel with tomato sauce, 274
carpaccio pizza with bresaola and salad, 46
carrot, escarole and zucchini tart, 264
cauliflower and cherry tomato focaccia, 186
cecina, 376
chapati, 374
cherry tomato and mushroom pizza, 22
chicken tacos with guacamole, 340
chicken, sweet corn and lentil pie, 218
chickpea crêpes with green salad, 314
chickpea crêpes with winter squash, 344
corn focaccia with pancetta, 162
couscous tart with feta, 252
crispy piadinas with crab salad, 298
crispy rosemary flatbread, 372
crostini with prosciutto and mushrooms, 290

d
devil's pizza, 30

e
eggplant and goat's cheese tart, 204
eggplant, mozzarella and egg tart, 282
emmenthal and tomato tart, 268
endive and brie pizza, 138
erbazzone, 200
escarole and ricotta tart, 206

f
farro crêpes with onions and olives, 310
fennel and finocchiona crostini, 350
flatbreads stuffed with potatoes and pancetta, 318
flatbreads with lardo and rosemary, 346
focaccia with anchovies and zucchini flowers, 150

focaccia with cheese, 156
focaccia with ciccioli, 172
focaccia with mushrooms,
catalogna chicory and taleggio, 190
focaccia with red onions and thyme, 176
four cheese pizza, 38
four seasons pizza, 16
fried bread, 306
fried chickpea focaccias, 158
fried pumpkin tortelli, 338
fried spinach ravioli, 296

g
genoa-style calzone, 74

h
ham and porcini pizza, 96
ham pizza, 14
ham, cheese and fried egg sandwiches, 352

l
liguria-style focaccia, 146
lucana pizza with pecorino and basil, 116

m
margherita pizza, 26
marinara pizza, 20
marinated octopus pizza, 60
meatball sandwiches with olive spread, 358
mediterranean crostoni, 286
mini focaccia panini with grilled vegetables, 360
mini panini with speck and artichokes, 288
mini potato focaccias with lardo and rosemary, 322
miniature buckwheat focaccias with fennel seeds, 170
miniature focaccias
with goat's cheese and vegetables, 178
mixed seafood pizza, 34
mozzarella in carrozza, 292
mushroom and arugula pizza, 110
mushroom and goat's cheese rolls, 328

n
neapolitan pizza, 28

o
olive and onion pizza, 64
olive bread with gruyère, 224
olive pizza with fresh tomatoes, 132
onion schiacciata, 174

p
panini with bresaola,
cherry tomatoes and parmesan, 300
panzerotti with prosciutto and gruyère, 326
panzerotti with provola and sausage, 330
parma-style fritters, 368
pear and gorgonzola pizza, 48
phyllo tart with zucchini and escarole, 230
piadina romagnola, 378
piadinas with prosciutto, buffalo mozzarella,
grilled tomatoes and basil, 354
piadinas with swiss chard and scamorza, 336
pineapple and prosciutto pizza, 90

Analytical Index

pizza bianca, 42
pizza marinara with mussels, 62
pizza with fontina, ricotta and cherry tomatoes, 134
pizza with french fries, 142
pizza with onions and cannellini beans, 140
pizza with pecorino, fresh porcini and ham, 54
pizza with smoked provola and asparagus, 118
pizza with sweet corn, arugula and parmesan, 130
pizza with tuna and zucchini flowers, 100
pizza with walnuts and brie, 120
polenta bread with sausage, 370
potato and asiago quiche, 228
potato and pancetta pizza, 76
potato and porcini quiche, 234
potato and porcini strudel, 270
potato focaccia with gorgonzola and marjoram, 152
potato focaccia with rosemary, 154
potato-thyme focaccia, 166
prosciutto and artichoke pizza, 70
prosciutto pizza, 18
provençal focaccia, 182
puff pastry tart with feta, 210
puglian focaccia, 160
pumpkin flatbread with leek and tofu, 240

q

quiche lorraine, 258

r

radicchio and scamorza calzone, 66
radicchio and winter squash tart, 262
red pizza with bresaola and fennel, 92
ricotta and prosciutto panzerotti, 320
robiola, salmon and dill tart, 250
russian pizza, 72

s

salt cod and broccoli pie, 272
sausage and mushroom pizza, 32
sautéed artichoke and chicken liver crostini, 332
savory cheesecake, 236
savory ham, olive and gruyère pie, 246
savory pear and parmesan strudel, 278
savory pizza, 98
savory potato and bacon tart, 256
savory pumpkin and chickpea strudel, 220
savory ricotta and salami pie, 232
savory san vito tart, 222
savory spinach bread with feta, 216
savory tart with peas, olives and pine nuts, 208
savory tart with ricotta, herbs and fresh tomatoes, 238
savory zucchini, tomato and fontina tart, 280
schiaccia with onions and anchovies, 164
shrimp, olive and arugula pizza, 82
smoked salmon pizza, 58
spiced beef triangles, 342
spicy onion and olive pizza, 128

spinach and grana tart, 214
spinach and swiss chard savory tart, 276
spinach crescioni, 226
squash tart with pumpkin seeds, 212
stuffed focaccia with artichokes and finocchiona, 192
stuffed focaccia with broccoli and sausage, 194
stuffed focaccia with ricotta and nettles, 148
stuffed focaccia with ricotta, cherry tomatoes and basil, 168
stuffed focaccia with tomatoes and anchovies, 196
stuffed herb focaccia with spinach and pancetta, 188
summer kamut pizza, 52
sweet and sour crostini, 304
swiss chard tart, 254

t

tigelle, 308
tomato and tuma ravioli, 334
truffled leek panzerotti, 364
truffled pizza with sausage, 80
truffled squash pizza, 84
tuna and potato pizza, 78
tyrolean pizza, 68

u

urbino-style focaccia, 180

v

vegetable and mozzarella pizza, 126
vegetable tart with raisins and pine nuts, 242
vesuvian strudel, 260

w

walnut and pecorino rolls, 316
white pizza with anchovies and capers, 36
white pizza with asparagus and bottarga, 50
white pizza with asparagus and cherry tomatoes, 136
white pizza with truffle oil, 114

z

zighini pizza, 102
zucchini and pecorino tart tatin, 244
zucchini and smoked salmon panini, 294
zucchini tart with goat's cheese and pancetta, 202
zucchini, potato and ricotta tart, 248

Pizza & Co.

First Published in the USA in 2008 by
Fireside
an imprint of Simon&Schusters
1230 Avenue of the Americas
New York, NY 10020
USA

Published originally under the title "Pizza & Co."
© 2005 Food Editore srl
Via Bordoni, 8 - 20124 MILAN
Via Mazzini, 6 - 43100 PARMA
www.foodeditore.it

English Translation
Traduzioni Culinarie

Photographs
Alberto Rossi and Davide Di Prato

Recipes
Simone Rugiati and Licia Cagnoni

Printed in China in 2008